MED[ICAL] MANAGEMENT OF DEPRESSION

by

Charles DeBattista, D.M.H., M.D.
Assistant Professor
Director, Depression Clinic
Department of Psychiatry and
Behavioral Sciences
Stanford University School of Medicine
Stanford, California

edited by

Ira David Glick, M.D.
Professor of Psychiatry
Department of Psychiatry and
Behavioral Sciences
Stanford University School of Medicine
Stanford, California

Medical Management of Depression

— Direct Mail Orders —
EMIS, Inc.
P.O. Box 1607
Durant, OK 74702-1607

— Telephone Orders —
1-800-225-0694
— FAX Your Order —
(405) 924-9414

Published in the United States of America 1997

ISBN: 0-929240-70-7

– TABLE OF CONTENTS –

— TABLES —

— FIGURES —

Acknowledgements

This book would not have been possible without the patience of my wife Sandy, and the efforts of my colleagues in the Mood Disorders Clinic in the Department of Psychiatry and Behavioral Sciences at Stanford University.

Proofreading by Kim Cox, Jeanne Ann Breen, Dr. Mehmet Sofuoglu and Betsy Nilson were much appreciated. Ms. Nilson also organized and prepared the later drafts of the text. Dr. Ira Glick's editing and suggestions were invaluable in producing a coherent discussion.

Finally, I am grateful to Alan F. Schatzberg whose kind mentoring over the recent years provided both the foundation and the inspiration for this manuscript.

Illustrator

Pearce Geotz

– OTHER CENTER INDEX PUBLICATIONS –

Available from:

EMIS, Inc.

REPRODUCTIVE HEALTH

Breastfeeding: *A Problem-Solving Manual* - 4th ed. — Saunders, Carroll & Johnson
Contraceptive Surgery for Men and Women - 2nd ed. — Moss/AVSC
Endometriosis: *The Enigmatic Disease* — Corson
Estrogen Replacement Therapy User Guide - 2nd ed. — Gambrell
Gynecological Care Manual for HIV Positive Women — Denenberg
Hormone Replacement Therapy - 4th ed. — Gambrell
Managing Contraceptive Pill Patients - 8th ed. — Dickey
Managing Danazol Patients - 2nd ed. — Dickey
Menopause: *Clinical Concepts* - 2nd ed. — London & Chihal
Oral Contraceptive User Guide - 2nd ed. — Dickey
Safer Sex: *A Guide To Condoms* - 2nd ed. — Brackett

CARDIOLOGY

Cholesterol Treatment: *User Guide To Lipid Disorder Management* - 2nd ed. — Leaf
Emergency Cardiac Maneuvers - 2nd ed. — Bartecchi
Hypertension Treatment User Guide - 2nd ed. — Kaplan
Management of Heart Failure — Cohn & Kubo
Management of Hypertension -6 th ed. — Kaplan

GENERAL MEDICINE

A Manual On Drug Dependence — Nahas
A Practical Anesthesia Information Guide — Jerome
Arthritis Therapy: *A Clinician's Manual* — Kantor
Assessment and Management of the Suicidal Adolescent - Clayton
Breast Disease In Women and Men — Shuler
Handbook of Headache Disorders - 2nd ed. — Elkind
Management of Aneurysmal Subarachnoid Hemorrhage — Fosset
Management of Diabetes Mellitus - 3rd ed. — Schwartz
Mid-Life Sexuality: *Enrichment and Problem Solving* — Semmens
Projective Psychodiagnostic Assessment — Caldwell & Dixon

EDUCATION

Chief Executive Officer's Guide For Health Facility Development - 2nd ed. – Weeks
Children With Special Needs - 2nd ed. — Bradway & Block
Resilience Enhancement For The Resident Physician — Messner*
Travel Well – *a gourmet guide to healthy travel* – Kaplan *

*Not Center-Indexed Publications

Introduction

Major depression represents one of the most common disorders encountered in both general medical and psychiatric clinics. According to the National Co-Morbidity Study, the lifetime risk for developing major depression in America is 17.1 percent, with approximately six percent of the population, or 11 million people, depressed at any given time. Depressive symptoms are common among patients seeing general physicians, with up to 41 percent expressing symptoms of depression in the previous six months.

Depression is neither a transient illness nor a benign one. Approximately 20 percent of major depressive episodes continue for two years or longer, with the average untreated episode continuing from six to nine months. In addition, the chance of recurrence is high for major depression, with approximately 50 to 85 percent of patients having multiple recurrences. Worse still, approximately one in seven patients with untreated major depression ultimately takes his own life.

The economic cost of depression is enormous. Estimates of costs from lost work and productivity due to major depression range from $20 to $30 billion per year. When combined with the costs of treating depression and those resulting from suicide, it is clear that depression poses a considerable economic and emotional burden on society.

Unfortunately, primary care physicians frequently fail to diagnose this treatable disorder. Recent research suggests that primary care physicians are successful in detecting major depression less than 50 percent of the time. Psychiatrists often recognize the disorder, but treatments are evolving so quickly that many have difficulty keeping abreast of the most recent treatment approaches.

This text, *Medical Management of Depression*, is intended to provide a framework for approaching patients with major depression. As primary care physicians, nurse practitioners, and physician's assistants take larger roles in health care, they will increasingly be called upon to evaluate and treat psychiatric disorders. Historically, most psychotropic drugs, including antidepressants, are prescribed by non-psychiatric physicians, and this will continue to be the case. Thus, it appears more important than ever that primary care physicians and allied health professionals be knowledgeable about the assessment and treatment of major depression.

The final four sections of the book deal with treating special patient populations having major depression, including:

- Suicidal patients
- Geriatric and pediatric patients
- Patients with subtypes of depression such as psychotic depression
- Patients who are treatment resistant

Primary care clinicians may find these discussions less relevant than will practicing psychiatrists.

It is hoped that, while this book briefly reviews the continually growing number of medical options for assessment and treatment of major depression, all clinicians who treat the disorder will find aspects of these discussions relevant to their practices.

1.

#1 Diagnosis of Major Depression

Like all medical illness, major depression is associated with a constellation of signs and symptoms that characterize the disorder. Unfortunately, as with all psychiatric illnesses, major depression does not yet have reliable laboratory studies, such as blood tests or brain scans, to corroborate diagnosis. Psychological testing may add some support to the suspicion of major depression, but diagnosis rests largely on clinical interviews and patient histories. The criteria for diagnosis used by most clinicians is set forth in the *Diagnostic and Statistical Manual of Mental Disorders* (DSM IV) (see Table 1.1).

The DSM IV criteria consists of a group of signs and symptoms of at least two weeks' duration. These criteria are different from the frequent nonspecific complaint of "I'm depressed" and have important prognostic and treatment implications for clinicians. However, making a reliable diagnosis of major depression is not as simple as checking off a list of symptoms. The features of a major depressive episode may vary considerably from patient to patient as a function of a number of factors, including:

- Age
- Gender
- Cultural background (e.g., in many cultures, adult males are more likely to admit to sleep and appetite disturbances than to a depressed mood)

Also, individual signs and symptoms of major depression are not particularly specific and may be found in a number of normal and non-psychiatric conditions. Therefore, adequate diagnostic assessment involves:

- Viewing the signs and symptoms within the historical context in which they have evolved
- Assessing the impacts of these signs and symptoms on patient functioning
- Excluding other conditions that may be responsible for the clinical presentation

Signs of Major Depression

Most of the DSM IV criteria for major depression involve subjective complaints that must be elicited from patients. However, major depression also is characterized by a number of signs or more objective data that may be evident in the first few minutes of the clinical visit, including:

- The affect (emotional expression) associated with depressed mood
- Psychomotor retardation and/or agitation
- Decreased attentiveness
- Weight loss
- Diminished personal hygiene
- Slowed verbal response
- Scars of previous suicide attempts

Patients with major depression, particularly in its more serious forms, usually have an affect that reflects the mood. As a depressive episode progresses, smiling becomes less and less frequent and the range of emotional expression becomes more restricted. It may become impossible for depressed patients to laugh at jokes or even feign happiness. Their brows may furrow in a continual reflection of distress, and they frequently appear to be preoccupied and distracted. Crying episodes may begin and become difficult

TABLE 1.1 – **DSM IV Criteria for Major Depressive Episode**

A. Five or more of the symptoms listed below have been present during the same two-week period and represent a change from previous functioning; at least one of the symptoms is either depressed mood or loss of interest or pleasure.

(1) Depressed mood most of the day nearly every day, as indicated either by subjective report (e.g., feels sad or empty) or observations of others (e.g., appears tearful). Note: In children and adolescents, can be irritable mood
(2) Markedly diminished interest or pleasure in all, or almost all, activities most of the day nearly every day, as indicated by subjective account or observations of others
(3) Significant weight loss when not dieting or weight gain (e.g., a change of more than five-percent body weight) in one month or decrease or increase in appetite nearly every day. Note: In children, failure to achieve expected weight gains
(4) Insomnia or hypersomnia nearly every day
(5) Psychomotor agitation or retardation nearly every day, as indicated not merely by subjective feelings of restlessness or being slowed down but by observations of others
(6) Fatigue or loss of energy nearly every day

(7) Feelings of worthlessness or excessive or inappropriate guilt (which may be delusional) nearly every day, as indicated not merely by self-reproach or guilt about being sick
(8) Diminished ability to think or concentrate or indecisiveness nearly every day, as indicated either by subjective account or observations of others
(9) Recurrent thoughts of death (not just fear of dying), recurrent suicidal ideation without a specific plan, or a suicide attempt or a specific plan for committing suicide

B. The symptoms do not meet criteria for a mixed episode.

C. The symptoms cause clinically significant distress or impairment in social, occupational, or other important areas of functioning.

D. The symptoms are not due to the direct physiological effects of a substance (e.g., an abused drug, a medication) or a general medical condition (e.g., hypothyroidism).

E. The symptoms are not better accounted for by bereavement (i.e., after the loss of a loved one) or the symptoms persist for longer than two months or are characterized by marked functional impairment, morbid preoccupation with worthlessness, suicidal ideation, psychotic symptoms, or psychomotor retardation.

(Reprinted with publisher's permission)

to control; such episodes may be precipitated by seemingly minor provocations, such as the clinician asking the patient how he is feeling or by an expression of sympathy that the patient is not feeling well. Some patients, however, are so depressed that they cannot cry; they describe a numbness and show an extremely restricted range of emotions. While a depressed affect may not be evident in all patients suffering from a major depressive episode, it is frequently the first clue about the nature of the problem.

Psychomotor agitation is found in about 70 percent of females and 50 percent of males with major depression. In its mildest forms, it is evidenced by patients' fidgeting with their hair or personal belongings and their having to change positions continually while sitting. One leg may bounce nervously, or patients may tap anxiously on arm rests. In more severe cases, patients literally may not be able to sit down; pacing becomes a way of binding some of the anxiety. Hand wringing also may evidence the profound distress these patients are experiencing.

Psychomotor retardation, a slowing motor activity and thought process, is present in approximately 50 percent of patients having a major depressive episode. It often begins with a minor decrease in the amplitude and volume of speech, forcing the clinician to repeat questions because answers are mumbled or barely audible.

Patients also may be slow to reply to questions, pausing for uncomfortably long periods before speaking. Patients often tend to slump and be relatively immobile, and their eye contact with clinicians is often limited as they gaze at the floor or wall during interviews. Their gaits may be noticeably slowed; and, if offered a handshake, they may be slow to respond. In general, it may appear as if patients' batteries have run down and all motor activity has been compromised.

Other signs of depression may be evident in patients who are followed over time. Anorexia, for example, is frequently accompanied by weight loss; patients appear thinner, their clothes do not fit as well, and, in severe cases, patients may be cachectic to the point of requiring a feeding tube.

Patients' lack of motivation and interest is commonly reflected by diminished interest in personal appearance. Patients who typically have looked as though they've stepped from fashion pages may begin to present in a somewhat disheveled manner. They may miss regularly scheduled appointments because they lack the motivation and energy to maintain their regular routines.

Patients who present with previous suicide attempts are a particularly worrisome group. Evidence of previous suicide attempts represent a history of emotional distress and may reflect a history of serious depression. There may be scars on the anterior aspect of their left wrists (in right-handed patients) from wrist-slashing attempts, rope burns on their necks from previous hanging attempts, or even gunshot trauma from self-inflicted wounds. Any suggestion of self-inflicted trauma, past or current, should be explored in detail.

Symptoms of Major Depression

The symptoms of major depression outlined in DSM IV (Table 1.1) include disturbances of:

- Mood
- Sleep

- Appetite
- Energy
- Cognition
- Motivation
- Interest

In addition, thoughts of death are present in many patients. While the DSM IV criteria require that a combination of five or more symptoms, including depressed mood or lack of interest, be present for at least two weeks, many patients will have been depressed considerably longer before they seek treatment. On occasion, symptoms may have been present for years before patients recognize that something is wrong and decide to seek solutions.

Depressed mood is an almost universal symptom of major depression, but the signs of a depressed mood may not be evident. Some patients may be unwilling to admit to a depressed mood secondary to social or cultural factors (such as the stigma associated with psychiatric illness). Most patients, however, will confirm a depressed mood when specifically asked about it. Depressed patients will typically describe a trend towards worsening sadness, sometimes associated with a sense of hopelessness. Irritability may also be endorsed by the patient; patients are less tolerant or more easily annoyed when depressed than when not.

Anhedonia, a loss of interest or pleasure in usual activities, is perhaps the second most common symptom of depression. More than 90 percent of patients in a major depressive episode indicate that life seems less interesting and enjoyable than previously. Workaholics lose their zeal for work, and avid fishermen can no longer be coaxed to cast a line; completing even a small task seems to involve a Herculean effort. Loss of libido is present in 60 percent of patients and may be part of the general anhedonia that depressed patients experience. As patients become more depressed, their sex lives are often among the first things to suffer. Frequency of sexual activity diminishes and often ceases, though sexual function is typically spared.

Fatigue is a symptom of major depression in about 80 percent of men and 90 percent of women. Patients complain of not having the energy to initiate tasks and of tiring easily once tasks are begun. Some depressed patients spend most of their time in bed because they genuinely feel too fatigued to dress and bathe and activities that require even minimal effort become too exhausting to initiate. It is sometimes difficult to discern whether patients are unproductive because of a lack of interest or because of decreased energy. Though the distinction is probably of little importance, both scenarios are problems for most patients and both problems respond to effective treatment.

The loss of or increase in appetite is present in 80 percent of patients suffering from major depression, with anorexia (appetite loss) appearing more typically. Early in a depressive episode, some patients suggest that food does not taste good or is tasteless and may complain of constipation and dull abdominal aches as the gut slows down with the rest of the body. It may be increasingly difficult for patients to force themselves to eat; in fact, some patients stop eating altogether. Atypical are patients who console themselves with food. They may experience carbohydrate cravings and actually show a weight gain.

Sleep disturbance is endorsed by 80 percent of depressed patients. Although early morning awakening (and not being able to fall back asleep) is the classic sleep disturbance in major depression, difficulty falling asleep initially is perhaps more common; middle insomnia, frequent interruptions in sleep, is also common. Some patients suggest that they would feel much better if they could just get a full night of sleep, and this is often true.

Also common is hypersomnia, in which patients may require up to twice the amount of sleep they normally do. All depressed patients should be questioned regarding:

- The time they go to bed
- How long it takes them to fall asleep
- Whether their sleep is interrupted
- The time they wake up in the morning
- If this situation represents a change from their usual sleep patterns
- If this situation does represent a change, what the specific differences are

Guilt, or a feeling of worthlessness, is present in about 70 percent of depressed patients and is often overlooked in clinical assessments. Depressed males often lament disappointing their families because they are no longer productive and feel they are burdens, or they may recall past transgressions for which they feel the need to be punished. Sometimes feelings of guilt may reach delusional proportions, with patients believing they are responsible for the problems of their families, of their employers, or perhaps even of society.

Among the most alarming symptoms of patients in the throes of a major depressive episode are thoughts of death or suicidal ideation. Approximately 80 percent of depressed patients endorse suicidal thoughts; the lifetime risk of patients ultimately taking their own lives is estimated at 15 percent. For most depressed patients, suicidal thoughts are of a passive quality. Depressed patients may hope to die while falling asleep or to contract a serious illness so they will not have to go on living. As the depression progresses, however, these thoughts may take on a more active form and suicide may seem like an increasingly viable option. Seriously depressed patients may begin to devise specific plans to end their lives and may make attempts to do so. The potentially suicidal patient requires careful evaluation and aggressive treatment (see Section #13).

A number of symptoms common to major depression are not specifically listed in the DSM IV criteria. Anxiety, for example, is endorsed by the vast majority of depressed patients and may be reflected in psychomotor agitation. Depressed patients typically complain of feeling high-strung and unable to relax. This anxiety may contribute to their difficulty to concentrate and, subsequently, with the short-term memory problems that plague most depressed patients.

Hypochondriacal concerns are seen in about 30 percent of depressed patients, particularly the elderly. Patients may believe or hope they feel bad because of some serious non-psychiatric physical disorder that has not yet been discovered. Hypochondriacal concerns may take on a delusional quality; for example, depressed patients may believe they feel bad because of an undiscovered brain tumor, and such beliefs can persist despite reassurances to the contrary.

Rarer in depressed patients is derealization and depersonalization. Depressed patients sometimes complain that things seem unfamiliar or unreal to them. Though they are frightened by these situations, patients tend to be easily reassured that such symptoms are sometimes seen during depression and anxiety states.

Since different people experience major depression differently, each patient may present with different signs and symptoms and still meet the criteria for depression. The important factor in assessment and subsequent diagnosis is the clinicians' attentiveness in looking for clues of a major depressive episode and in taking the time necessary to follow leads that suggest a major depression.

Diagnostic Interviews

There are as many ways to perform a diagnostic interview for depression as there are clinicians. Effective interviews, however, have some common features, the most important of which is attentive listening, since patients frequently reveal the nature of their difficulties if given the opportunity. The second most important feature is thoroughness. A diagnostic interview should include detailed histories of:

- How patients' complaints evolved
- When symptoms began
- How symptoms affect patients' abilities to function

Additional crucial elements of diagnostic interviews are:

- Psychiatric history
- Medical history
- Social history
- Family history

As with most interviews, it is generally desirable for clinicians to begin with open-ended questions and follow with closed questions, avoiding "yes" and "no" questions except in the most compromised patients. Restrictive questions may lead to certain interviewer biases or to predetermined conclusions.

Some useful open-ended screening questions to determine common symptoms of a major depressive episode include:

1. **How would you describe your mood or spirits recently?**
   If patients give a general response such as "not good," this can be pursued by asking them to say more about not feeling good. After patients have been given an opportunity to answer, specific inquiries may be pursued such as whether they feel sad and, if so, how much of the time. Patients with major depression feel sad most of the day every day; transient sadness may be within the normal range or secondary to another psychiatric condition, such as a personality disorder.
2. **When you wake up most mornings, how do you feel about facing the day?**
   Depressed patients usually dread facing the day. Frequently mornings are the worst time of day for severely depressed patients (diurnal variation), who often lack the energy and motivation to tackle the chores of day-to-day living.
3. **Do you ever feel that life is not worth living?**
   Many people respond positively to this question, so it is important to ask patients to speak about this feeling. If they have persistent thoughts that life is not worth the struggle, it is crucial to focus the interview on any plans of

suicide, actual intent, means to commit suicide, and other risk factors for suicide (see Section #13).

4. **How have your sleep and appetite been?**
   It is important to differentiate acute disturbances from chronic sleep and appetite difficulties. Sleep should be characterized according to what time patients go to bed, how long it takes them to fall asleep (initial insomnia), whether they have interruptions in their sleep (middle insomnia), and what time they wake up. Appetite changes should be correlated to any weight losses or gains.
5. **How is your ability to concentrate and remember things?**
   If patients describe recent cognitive problems, several tests may be useful. Presenting patients three objects and asking them to recall the objects five minutes later, for example, is a simple and crude measure of recent memory. Attention also may be assessed by such mental status tasks as presenting patients with seven digits and having them recall the digits immediately, having them subtract from 100 by sevens, and asking them to spell the word "world" backwards. Depressed patients frequently perform poorly on tests of concentration and subsequently do poorly on tests of recent memory.
6. **What is your opinion of yourself?**
   Feelings of worthlessness are not universal, but most depressed patients are somewhat self-deprecating. The depressed patient may claim that he is not worthy of his family's affection. Furthermore, despite a solid job performance, he may conclude that he is such

a poor worker that his employer should terminate him. While not all depressed patients feel worthless, most patients who feel worthless are probably depressed.

7. **What do you believe the future holds for you?**
   This question taps into feelings of hopelessness. Almost uniformly, depressed patients tend to feel pessimistic about the future and may have a distorted sense of the past. Patients in the throes of a major depressive episode, may report that their lives have always been miserable. Once the depression resolves, patients may tell a different story. This question also may elicit nihilistic concerns. Patients may feel they are doomed and that the future can only bring death.
8. **Have you been feeling critical of yourself for things you have done or for not doing things you feel you should have done?**
   Guilt can take many forms; among the most common is that of patients feeling they are disappointing their loved ones. This feeling occurs because depression reduces a person's ability to function and relate to others. Oppressive guilt about past transgressions is somewhat less common and may be so overstated as to be delusional.

Depending on the skill and experience of interviewers, reliable diagnostic assessments can take a short period of time. However, confidence in diagnoses increases with the amount of time spent with patients. Reliable diagnoses are perhaps best made from several visits with patients since symptoms may fluctuate considerably over time and what initially appears to be a severe depressive episode may seem but a minor disturbance the following week. However, severe symptoms should be taken seriously, even if they are episodic.

Use of Depression Questionnaires and Scales

A number of questionnaires used as screening devices to detect depression are available. The most popular is the Beck Depression Inventory (BDI) that is completed by the patient. The advantage of the BDI is that it can raise the suspicion of a major depressive episode in only a few minutes; a score above 16 is associated with moderate to severe depression. The scale, however, is not a substitute for the diagnostic interview; even a brief interview with a patient is likely to produce far more information than such scales do. On the other hand, this inventory can be used both as an initial screening device and as a tool to assess symptoms and clinical improvement over time.

Another commonly used scale is the Hamilton Depression Scale (Ham-D), which typically consists of 17 to 24 items that measure the signs and symptoms of depression. The Ham-D tends to be weighted more heavily to vegetative symptoms, such as sleep disturbance and weight changes, and requires clinicians to ask patients about each of the items. A complete Ham-D assessment may take 20 minutes or more. While it is commonly used in antidepressant research, its major use in clinical settings may be in following patients' progress. A score of 20 or above is usually indicative of a major depressive episode; scores of less than eight reliably suggest complete remission.

Communicating the Diagnosis

It may be difficult for many patients to accept the diagnosis of depression, since depression carries with it the stigma of psychiatric illness. Depressed patients may be invested in the idea that something is physically wrong with them and may think a diagnosis of depression means "It's all in your head; there's nothing wrong with you."

Patients may be better able to accept the diagnosis if the announcement is framed within another context. One common approach is to describe depression as a medical illness that has a biochemical cause and runs a specific time course. It should be emphasized to patients that depression is a common illness suffered by millions of Americans and that, fortunately, it can be treated effectively. It also may be suggested that people are no more responsible for developing major depression than they are for developing diabetes or other medical problems. Drawing on the similarity of major depression to other medical illnesses may make the diagnosis more palatable for some patients.

A related strategy is to reframe the diagnosis of depression in terms of stress. Most patients understand the concept of stress and are able to acknowledge that stress may be affecting them in some way. Clinicians may suggest that, as stress accumulates, the body becomes worn down and depressed and, as a result, sleep, appetite, energy, and thinking become compromised. The nature of depression can then be discussed in more detail.

Additionally, it helps for supportive friends or family members of patients to be present when the diagnosis is made. Family members can become allies in patients' treatments and help patients process the information.

Patients also may be provided with brochures and other literature about major depression. These are extremely valuable tools to support clinicians' diagnosis and treatment.

References:

American Psychiatric Association: The diagnostic and statistical manual of mental disorders, 4th ed. APA Press, Washington, DC, 1994.

Andreason NC: Affective disorders: Concepts, diagnosis, and classification. In: Handbook of affective disorders. Paykel ES. Guilford Press, New York, 1982.

Beck AT: Depression: Clinical, experimental, and theoretical aspects. Harper and Row, New York, 1967.

Clark DC, Cavenaugh S, Gibbons RD: The core symptoms of depression in medical and psychiatric patients. J Nerv Mental Disorders 1983;171:705-713.

Hamilton WA: Rating scale for depression. J Neurology, Neurosurgery, and Psychiatry 1960;23:56-62.

Kaplan B, Sadock J: The comprehensive textbook of psychiatry, 5th ed. Williams and Wilkins, Baltimore, 1991.

Rush AJ: Clinical diagnosis of depression. Clin Chem 1988;34:814-821.

Rush AJ: Problems associated with the diagnosis of depression. J Clin Psychiatry, June 1990;51:6 (suppl)15-22.

Stokes PE: A primary care perspective on the management of acute and long-term depression. J Clin Psychiatry, Aug. 1993;(suppl)54(8):74-84.

Tollefson, GD: Recognition and treatment of major depression. Family Practice, Nov. 1990;(suppl) 59S-69S.

#2 Differential Diagnosis of Depression

2. The signs and symptoms of major depression are sufficiently nonspecific that, individually, they may encompass a variety of normal states, psychiatric disorders, and non-psychiatric medical conditions. Therefore, accurate diagnosis of major depression depends, in part, on excluding conditions with which depression may be confused. Differential diagnosis is essential not only for making an adequate diagnosis of major depression but also for planning appropriate treatment.

Differentiating Major Depression From Normal States

Sadness and dysphoria (feeling bad) are integral parts of the human experience. It is appropriate and expected that patients will sometimes feel sad or bad. Moreover, unpleasant emotional states are probably adaptive to our well being, in that we are motivated to avoid actions that are likely to increase a dysphoric state. For example, we go to work partly because, if we did not, the consequences might make us feel bad (such as being fired).

In lay terms, depression is often used as a synonym for feeling sad or dysphoric. The syndrome of major depression, however, is not synonymous with these emotional states. Unpleasant emotional states like sadness usually:

- Occur in the context of a specific situation or stress
- Are transient
- Are rarely incapacitating

While major depression may also occur in the context of a specific situation, it:

- Is persistent
- Disrupts patients' abilities to function
- Tends to have a life of its own once it begins

If a major depressive major episode is triggered by a financial loss, for example, the depression is unlikely to vanish if a lost fortune is suddenly regained.

In addition, major depression is characterized by distressing vegetative symptoms that are not part of normal sadness or dysphoria, such as:

- Changes in appetite
- Sleep disturbances
- Energy problems

Grief is the normal reaction to the loss of a loved one, and, unlike transient sadness, may be accompanied by sleep and appetite disturbances. Grief may differ in clinical presentation from typical major depression by the relative absence of psychomotor retardation and suicidal thoughts. Furthermore, while patients may grieve over the death of a loved one forever, it is usual for patients to be incapacitated by their grief for more than two to eight weeks. Thus, most clinicians choose to treat any grief reaction as a major depressive episode if it is characterized by:

- Suicidal thoughts
- Psychomotor retardation
- Two or more months' duration

Distinguishing Major Depression from Other Psychiatric Disorders

The clinical syndrome of major depression shares features with a variety of mood disorders and other psychiatric conditions. It may also arise

FIGURE 2.1 — **Algorithm for the Evaluation of Depressed Mood**

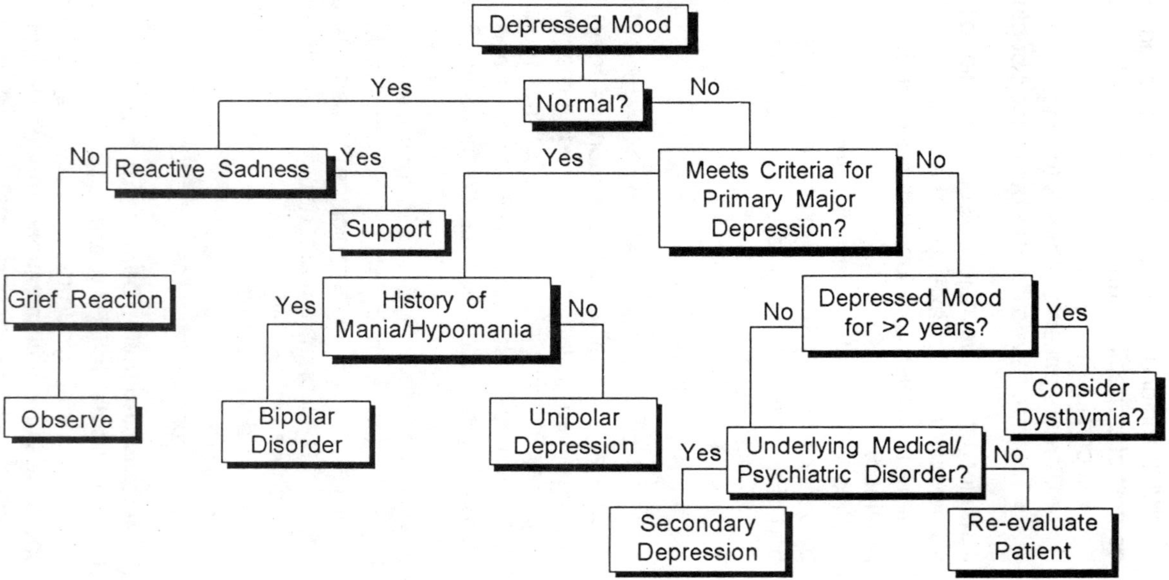

secondary to a primary psychiatric disorder, such as schizophrenia or obsessive compulsive disorder. Patients may become be so distressed by their psychotic symptoms or compulsions that they become demoralized and develop depressive symptoms. A secondary depression will often respond to the successful treatment of the primary disorder.

Major depression is in the family of disorders called affective or mood disorders that share a difficulty with mood regulation as a central feature. Mood disorders are heterogeneous and respond to different treatments. Thus, major depression must be distinguished from other mood disorders.

Dysthymia, a related disorder seen in approximately three percent of the population, is frequently confused with major depression (see Table 2.1). It is a low-grade, chronic depression of at least two years' duration that does not quite meet the criteria for major depression.

Dysthymic patients frequently complain of a lifetime of milder problems with sleep disturbance and appetite as well as self-esteem difficulties. While dysthymia may alter patients' abilities to function, the social and vocational impact of dysthymia is usually less dramatic than in major depression. In addition, depressive symptoms appear to be part of patients' character structure rather than discrete depressive episodes. A major depression may be superimposed on the disorder (double depression), making treatment more difficult.

Psychotherapy has been the traditional treatment of choice for dysthymia, though data on efficacy have been scarce. There is growing data that antidepressants are quite useful in treating dysthymia.

TABLE 2.1 – **DSM IV Criteria for Dysthymia**

A. Depressed mood for most of the day for more days than not, as indicated either by subjective account or observation of others for at least two years. **<u>Note:</u>** In children and adolescents, mood can be irritable and duration must be at least one year.

B. Presence, while depressed, of two (or more) of the following:
   (1) Poor appetite or overeating
   (2) Insomnia or hypersomnia
   (3) Low energy or fatigue
   (4) Low self-esteem
   (5) Poor concentration or difficulty making decisions
   (6) Feelings of hopelessness

C. During the past two-year period (one year for children or adolescents) of the disturbance, the person has never been without the symptoms in Criteria A and B for more than two months at a time.

D. No major depressive episode has been present during the first two years of the disturbance (one year for children and adolescents), i.e., the disturbance is not better accounted for by chronic major depressive disorder or major depressive disorder in partial remission.

E. There has never been a manic episode, a mixed episode, or a hypomanic episode; and criteria has not been met for cyclothymic (mood swing) disorder.

F. The disturbance does not occur exclusively during the course of a chronic psychotic disorder, such as schizophrenia or delusional disorder.

G. The symptoms are not due to the direct physiological effects of a substance (e.g., a drug of abuse or a medication) or a general medical condition (e.g., hypothyroidism).

H. The symptoms cause clinically significant distress or impairment in social, occupational, or other important areas of functioning.

(Reprinted with publisher's permission)

Bipolar disorder is considerably less common than major depression, with an incidence around one percent of the population. It is characterized by:

- Cycles of elevated or irritable mood
- A decreased need for sleep
- An increase in impulsive or goal-directed behavior (see Table 2.2)

Manic and hypomanic episodes (see Table 2.3) are usually, but not always, interspersed with depressive episodes. It is common for depressive episodes to predate the onset of manic episodes by many years. Thus, patients' major depressive episodes may evolve into bipolar illness over time. In addition, it may be difficult to distinguish a manic episode that has a significant component of agitation and dysphoria from an agitated depression. In some manic episodes, dysphoria may be as common as euphoria. The personal and family histories are usually the best data for distinguishing bipolar from unipolar depression. If patients have one clearly defined past manic or hypomanic episode, they are bipolar regardless of their current affective state. Antidepressants may substantially increase the risk of precipitating a manic episode in a depressed patient with bipolar illness, and mood-stabilizing agents, such as lithium, are frequently required for treatment.

Another class of disorders that share many features with major depression are anxiety disorders. Anxiety is a pervasive symptom of major depression, and depressed mood is a common secondary symptom of anxiety disorders. In fact, depression and anxiety disorders appear to have a close biological relationship and may exist on a continuum rather than as truly distinct entities. However, while many treatments effective for depression are also effective for anxiety disorders, the converse is not necessarily true. Benzodiazepines, such as diazepam, are the medications of choice in the treatment of generalized anxiety disorder but do not appear effective in resolving a major depressive episode. Thus, mistaking an anxiety disorder for major depression is likely to result in less than optimal treatment.

Several features may help distinguish anxiety disorders from depression. The first is chronology. In major depression, the agitation (sometimes confused with anxiety) follows the depressed mood. In an anxiety disorder, anxiety symptoms are evident first and are sometimes followed by a secondary depression. Sleep in anxiety disorders tends to be marked by difficulty falling asleep, while early morning awakening appears somewhat more common in major depression. Also, patients with major depression tend to wake up depressed; this tends not to be the case for anxiety disorders.

The sympathetic discharge in anxiety disorders may give a somewhat different flavor to the concomitant somatic symptoms. For example, gastrointestinal complaints in anxiety disorders might be more likely to involve indigestion, diarrhea, and gas, while constipation may be more common in major depression. Sympathetic discharge also may be more likely to cause problems with sexual function (i.e., premature ejaculation) than with libido.

Depressed mood in anxiety disorders tends to be more fleeting and fluctuating than in major depression.

TABLE 2.2 – **DSM IV Criteria for Manic Episode**

A. A distinct period of abnormally and persistently elevated, expansive, or irritable mood lasting at least one week (or any duration if hospitalization is necessary).

B. During the period of mood disturbance, three (or more) of the following symptoms have persisted (four if the mood is only irritable) and have been present to a significant degree:

(1) Inflated self-esteem or grandiosity
(2) Decreased need for sleep (e.g., feels rested after only three hours of sleep)
(3) More talkative than usual or pressure to keep talking
(4) Flight of ideas or subjective experience that thoughts are racing
(5) Distractibility (i.e., attention to or easily drawn to unimportant or irrelevant extemal stimuli)
(6) Increase in goal-directed activity (either socially, at work or school, or sexually) or psychomotor agitation
(7) Excessive involvement in pleasurable activities that have a high potential for painful consequences, e.g., engaging in unrestrained buying sprees, sexual indiscretions, or foolish business investments)

C. The symptoms do not meet criteria from mixed episode.

D. The mood disturbance is sufficiently severe to cause marked impairment in occupational functioning or in usual social activities or relationships with others or to necessitate hospitalization to prevent harm to self or others, or there are psychotic features.

E. The symptoms are not due to the direct physiological effects of a substance (e.g., a drug of abuse, a medication, or other treatment) or a general medical condition (e.g., hyperthyroidism).

<u>**Note:**</u> Manic-like episodes that are clearly caused by somatic antidepressant treatment (e.g., medication, electroconvulsive therapy, or light therapy) should not count toward a diagnosis of Bipolar I Disorder.

(Reprinted with publisher's permission)

TABLE 2.3 – **DSM IV Criteria for Hypomanic Episode**

A. A distinct period of persistently elevated, expansive, or irritable mood lasting at least four days that is clearly different from the usual nondepressed mood.

B. During the period of mood disturbance, three (or more) of the following symptoms have persisted (four if the mood is only irritable) and have been present to a significant degree:

(1) Inflated self-esteem or grandiosity
(2) Decreased need for sleep (e.g., feels rested after only three hours of sleep)
(3) More talkative than usual or pressure to keep talking
(4) Flight of ideas or subjective experiences that thoughts are racing
(5) Distractibility (i.e., attention to or easily drawn to unimportant or irrelevant external stimuli)
(6) Increase in goal-directed activity (either socially, at work or school, or sexually) or psychomotor agitation
(7) Excessive involvement in pleasurable activities that have a high potential for painful consequences (e.g., the person engages in unrestrained buying sprees, sexual indiscretions, or foolish business investments)

C. The episode is associated with an unequivocal change in functioning that is uncharacteristic of the person when not symptomatic.

D. The disturbance in mood and the change in functioning are observable by others.

E. The episode is not severe enough to cause marked impairment in social or occupational functioning or to necessitate hospitalization, and there are no psychotic features.

F. The symptoms are not due to the direct physiological effects of a substance (e.g., a drug of abuse, a medication, or other treatment) or a general medical condition (e.g., hyperthyroidism).

<u>**Note:**</u> Hypomanic-like episodes that are clearly caused by somatic antidepressant treatment (e.g., medication, electroconvulsive therapy, or light therapy) should not count toward a diagnosis of Bipolar II Disorder.

(Reprinted with publisher's permission)

Approximately five to 20 percent of patients with major depression will present with psychotic symptoms, including hallucinations and delusions. These so-called psychotic depressions are often confused with other psychotic disorders, including schizophrenia, brief reactive psychosis, and delusional disorders.

A distinguishing feature of psychotic depressions relative to other psychotic disorders is that, by definition, they occur in the context of a major depressive episode. These patients meet full criteria for major depression in addition to the psychotic symptoms (see Section #15).

Histories of psychotically depressed patients often provide clues of previous affective episodes. Patients with schizophrenia often have anhedonia, social withdrawal, and lack of motivation; but these tend to be a function of the underlying disorder and tend not to respond to antidepressants. The picture is further confused by the fact that approximately 30 percent of schizophrenic patients meet the criteria for major depression at some point in their illness and that a secondary depression may respond to antidepressant treatment. Careful review of personal histories, family histories, and psychiatric histories often help clarify the diagnosis. Psychological testing may also help distinguish psychotic depression from other psychotic disorders.

Psychotic depression may be treated effectively with electroconvulsive therapy and/or the combination of antidepressants and antipsychotic drugs. However, other psychotic disorders appear to be less responsive to these treatments.

While sleep disturbance is common in major depression, it also can exist as an independent sleep disorder, such as sleep apnea. Patients with sleep apnea may complain of significant middle insomnia and fatigue during the day, which may contribute to some dysphoria and problems with concentration. However, primary sleep disorders are rarely associated with other depressive symptoms, such as psychomotor retardation, guilt, or feelings of worthlessness.

Likewise, appetite disturbance may accompany other disorders or exist as an independent illness. Anorexia nervosa, in particular, is manifested by a dramatic loss of weight; patients with anorexia may be secondarily depressed. Nonetheless, if patients with eating disorders meet criteria for major depression, it is reasonable to treat the depression.

Depression Secondary to Non-Psychiatric Medical Factors

Depression Secondary to Medical Disorders

The list of organic disorders that may cause depressive symptoms such as fatigue, insomnia, and anorexia is almost inexhaustible. In addition, the rate of underlying physical illnesses that may be related to psychiatric disturbances in general is high. As many as 10 to 45 percent of psychiatric patients have underlying medical problems that may be related to their symptoms. However, several groups of disorders warrant special consideration because of their prevalence and association with depression.

Endocrine and metabolic disorders have long been associated with prominent psychiatric symptoms, particularly symptoms of depression. Among

TABLE 2.4 — **Nonpsychiatric Medical Conditions Associated with Symptoms of Depression**

Central Nervous System
- Dementia
- Epilepsy
- Head injury
- Multiple sclerosis
- Parkinson's disease
- Stroke

Nutritional Disorders
- Vitamin B_6 deficiency
- Vitamin B_{12} deficiency

Infectious Disorders
- AIDS
- Encephalitis
- Hepatitis
- Meningitis

Endocrine/Metabolic Disorders
- Cushing's disease
- Hyper/hypoglycemia
- Hypo/hyperthyroidism
- Hyponatremia
- Hypocalcemia

Malignant Cancer
- Pancreatic
- Small cell/lung

Autoimmune Disorders
- Large cell vasculitis
- Lupus

the most common endocrine disorders linked to depressive symptoms are those involving the thyroid, especially hypothyroidism found predominantly in women during middle and older age.

The most common psychiatric symptoms of hypothyroidism are:

- Fatigue
- Cognitive slowing with memory impairment
- Psychomotor retardation
- Anhedonia
- A mood that is perhaps more consistent with apathy and irritability than depression

Hypothyroidism may have an insidious onset, and the psychiatric symptoms may be more prominent than physical signs, usually:

- Dry rough skin
- Alopecia (hair loss)
- Slow, monotone speech
- Apathy
- Inertia
- Irritability
- Anxiety
- Depressed mood

Depressive symptoms, including crying spells, have been reported when a thyroidectomy results in hypoparathyroidism. Signs of profound hypocalcemia, such as carpopedal spasm and laryngeal stridor, may occur in only the most extreme cases of hypoparathyroidism.

Disorders in the production of cortisol are frequently accompanied by depressive symptoms. Cushing's disease (a disorder usually due to exogenous corticosteroids) is more common in women than men. Up to 50 percent of patients with this disorder have:

- Significant depressed mood
- Apathy
- Fatigue
- Truncal obesity (classical sign)
- Moon facies (classical sign)

Likewise, Addison's disease (adrenal insufficiency) is accompanied, in a significant percentage of patients, by:

- Memory loss
- Depressed mood
- Physical exhaustion

Addison's disease may be considered in the differential diagnosis of depression, particularly in young- to middle-aged males.

Neurological disorders constitute another major group of disorders frequently associated with depression. Approximately 40 percent of patients who suffer strokes develop depression. While some cases of depression following stroke are the result of patients having to face the devastating physical sequelae of a cerebrovascular infarction, depression may also emerge as a direct consequence of the anatomical insult. Studies have suggested that patients with left hemisphere frontal lesions have a greater likelihood of developing depression.

In some elderly patients, stroke may be signaled, even without motor or language difficulties, by:

- The sudden onset of depressed mood
- Difficulty concentrating
- Apathy

Neurological consultation with brain imaging should be considered in those depressed patients with any suggestion of:

- Motor impairment
- Language impairment

Distinguishing dementia from depression in the elderly can be a difficult problem. Depression may present with cognitive disturbance, including problems with memory and concentration, which can be pronounced in the elderly to the point that patients appear demented. A distinguishing feature of major depression is that the onset tends to be more rapid than in dementia. Also, depression is often, though not always, temporally related with some memory loss; and depressed patients are more likely to answer questions with "I don't know" rather than provide near misses on tests of memory and cognitive ability. In addition, depressed patients often complain bitterly of their difficulty with memory, while demented patients may be somewhat less aware of the extent of their difficulties. Finally, depressed patients tend to have more difficulties than demented patients with:

- Insomnia
- Anxiety
- Sex drive

Many patients who must contend with a life-threatening disorder, such as cancer, understandably become depressed, though depressive symptoms in some patients predate the actual diagnosis of cancer. Some retrospective studies, for example, describe the onset of depression occurring months before the diagnosis of pancreatic cancer. It is not unusual for some malignancies to present early with:

- Fatigue
- Malaise
- Weight loss

These symptoms are sometimes mistaken for major depression. The weight loss in depression may be extreme, but severe anorexia and weight loss in a middle-aged or elderly patient should be considered to be of organic etiology until proven otherwise.

Primary or secondary brain cancer can produce a variety of mental symptoms, including depression. Tumors in most of the supratentorial area have been implicated as potentially-causing depressive symptoms. Since many types of cancer commonly produce brain metastases (including lung, breast, gastrointestinal, and melanotic cancers), it is conceivable that the onset of depression in some cancer patients is directly related to the progress of the disease. Furthermore, some types of cancer, such as small-cell bronchogenic tumors, are implicated in the development of limbic encephalitis, which may present with multiple psychiatric and cognitive difficulties, including a mood disorder.

Vitamin deficiencies are sometimes a factor in the depressive syndromes seen in:

- Patients with gastric surgery
- The elderly
- Patients who abuse alcohol

Among the most common vitamin deficiencies reported in depressed patients are B_{12} (pernicious anemia) and folate deficiencies. The development of affective symptoms may predate other signs of a vitamin deficiency, such as a macrocytic anemia or dementia, by many months. Routine screening for vitamin B deficiencies is probably of doubtful value, except in those patients most at risk.

Depression Secondary to Concomitant Drugs

Many medications have been implicated as causes of major depression. It is unclear whether some of these drugs produce the anergy, fatigue, and dysphoria that is confused with major depression or whether some drugs actually produce the syndrome of major depression. Several classes of agents warrant special attention in evaluating histories of patients who present with depression.

One important group of drugs to consider is the antihypertensive group. There is substantial evidence that high blood pressure pills, taken by millions of Americans daily, may be problematic for depressed patients. Reserpine and methyldopa are among the oldest antihypertensives still in use, and both appear capable of inducing a major depressive episode. In one review, 20 percent of 725 patients on reserpine met criteria for a major depressive episode and one in 12 patients had severe depression. Reported with reserpine use are the symptoms of:

- Fatigue
- Hopelessness
- Insomnia
- Psychomotor retardation

Reserpine is responsible for the depletion of monoamine neurotransmitters, a depletion that has been implicated as central to the etiology of major depression. Methyldopa also depletes the monoamines serotonin and dopamine; high doses of the drug can result in depression in 10 percent of patients.

The role of beta-blockers in inducing depression is more controversial than the role of methyldopa (Aldomet) or reserpine (Hydropres). The

TABLE 2.5 — **Medications Implicated in Depressive Symptoms**

Cardiovascular Medications	***Steroids/Hormones***
Antiarrythmics	Estrogens
Beta-blockers	Glucocorticoids
Digitalis	Progesterone
Guanethidine	
Methyldopa	***Narcotics***
Reserpine	Meperidine
	Morphine
Central System Depressants	Pentazocine
Alcohol	
Barbiturates	***Other Drugs***
Benzodiazepines	Carbidopa-Levodopa
	Cimetidine
Withdrawal from Stimulant Drugs	Disulfiram
Amphetamine	
Cocaine	
Sympathomimetics	

incidence of depression in patients taking non-specific, lipophilic beta-blockers may be as high as 23 percent, but some studies have found no correlation between beta-blockers and major depression. It is unclear whether beta-blockers simply cause the anergy, fatigue, and listlessness that is confused with depression or whether they actually contribute to the pathophysiology of major depression, as do methyldopa and reserpine. Guanethidine, clonidine, and hydralazine also have been associated with depressive symptomatology but at lower rates than reserpine, methyldopa, and beta-blockers. Calcium channel blockers and angiotensin converting enzyme (ACE) inhibitors appear to be safe alternatives for depressed hypertensive patients.

The central nervous system depressants, including alcohol, benzodiazepines, and barbiturates, have all been implicated in depressive symptoms. Alcoholism has significant co-morbidity with major depression but usually follows rather than precedes depression. Some of this co-morbidity is attributed to depressed patients' self-medication with alcohol. An alternative explanation is that depression is a consequence of the havoc alcoholism wreaks on patient's lives. Alcohol, as a central nervous system depressant, may be directly involved in producing depressive symptoms, including fatigue and apathy. In any case, alcoholism is a significant complicating factor in major depression, and many experts advise detecting and treating the abuse problem before attempting to treat the depression.

There is controversial literature that suggests benzodiazepines, such as diazepam (Valium), are also capable of inducing depression. In several trials of Valium for the treatment of anxiety, there was an increase in depressive symptoms reported, including suicidal thoughts. However, few conclusions can be drawn from these studies because most of them:

- Used different criteria for diagnosing depression
- Were not placebo-controlled
- Were retrospective

It is clear that many patients treated with benzodiazepines and other central nervous system depressants such as barbiturates feel tired, listless, and disinterested. Thus, central nervous system depressant effects must be considered in the differential assessment of patients presenting with depressive symptoms.

Glucocorticoid steroids are often associated with depressive symptoms. Just as Cushing's disease may result in major depression, so can the use of exogenous steroids, such as prednisone. The incidence of depression with prednisone may be as high as 40 percent and is reversible once the drug is discontinued. Depression is perhaps the most common psychiatric side effect of steroid use, followed by hypomania and mania. The higher doses of steroids are more closely correlated with depression than doses below 40 mg per day. Nevertheless, there may be no reasonable alternative to steroids in patients with autoimmune disorders or end-stage chronic obstructive pulmonary disease. Fortunately, the depression secondary to steroid use does appear quite responsive to antidepressant drugs.

References:

Beers MH, Passman LJ: Antihypertensive medications and depression. Drugs 1990;40(6):792-799.

Brock CD, Simpson WM: Dementia, depression, or grief? The differential diagnosis. Geriatrics, Oct 1990;45(10):37-43.

Kirmayer LJ, Robbins JM, Dworkin M, Yaffe MJ: Somatization and the recognition of depression and anxiety in primary care. Am J Psychiatry, May 1993;150(5):734-741.

Lishman HS: Organic psychiatry: The psychological consequences of cerebral disorder. Blackwell Scientific Publications, Oxford, 1978.

Muser JD, Cloninger CR: Co-morbidity of anxiety and mood disorders. APA Press, Washington, DC, 1990.

Rodin G, Vorshart K: Depression in the medically ill: An overview. Am J Psychiatry 1986;143:696-705.

Smith BD, Salzman C: Do benzodiazepines cause depression? Hosp Comm Psychiatry, Nov 1991; 42(11):1101-1102.

Toffelson GD: Recognition and treatment of major depression. Family Practice, Nov 1990;(suppl): 59S-69S.

#3 Laboratory Studies in Depression

3. Given the large number of medical conditions with which depression may be confused, screening laboratory studies can play an important role in evaluating depressed patients. However, it is impractical and unnecessary for clinicians to perform an endless battery of tests in an attempt to rule out all possible diagnoses in the differential. These tests are quite costly and do not appear to increase the likelihood of detecting occult medical conditions in asymptomatic psychiatric patients substantially. A thorough review of systems, medical histories, and physical examinations is likely to produce a higher yield; and an extensive series of tests increases the likelihood of finding abnormalities that are not clinically significant.

A few simple tests, though, can greatly enhance clinicians' confidence that depression is not secondary to underlying medical disorders (see Table 3.1), especially for outpatients. Depressed inpatients tend to be more seriously ill and may require more extensive screening tests.

In addition to detecting occult medical conditions, some baseline tests may also be useful in anticipating which patients may have difficulties with a given class of antidepressant medications.

Urinalysis

The dipstick urinalysis is an inexpensive test of great utility in screening for medical problems that may be associated with depressive symptoms. Since a urinalysis is not costly and can demonstrate many disorders, it should probably be included in the screening studies of all depressed patients. Routine urinalysis may indicate:

TABLE 3.1 — **Suggested Cost-Effective Screening Tests in the Evaluation of all Patients with Major Depression**

Screening Tests:

1. *Urinalysis*
2. *CBC*
3. *BUN/creatinine*
4. *Serum glucose*
5. *Sensitive TSH,* especially in females over age 50 and patients with a family history of thyroid disease.

Expanded Screening Test Battery for Use in Specific Population:

1. *Electrolytes,* for patients over age 65, those on antihypertensive drugs, and those with acute mental status changes.
2. *EKG,* if tricyclic antidepressant treatment is anticipated.
3. *SGOT/SGPT,* for patients with a history of alcoholism and possibly as a baseline for patients who will be treated with SSRIs and TCAs.
4. *Total Protein,* for any malnourished, depressed patients and perhaps in anticipation of pharmacotherapy.

- Renal disease
- Hepatobiliary problems
- Diabetes

The screening identifies a number of important components, including:

- Urine pH—which measures acidity of the urine, which can be elevated as a result of:
  - Severe anorexia
  - Starvation associated with depression
- Urine glucose – Which is useful in identifying the hyperglycemia of diabetes
- Urine bilirubin – Which can be elevated when the hepatic biliary system is obstructed
- Specific gravity – Which gives some indication of the kidney's ability to concentrate urine. A high specific gravity means the urine is concentrated, a condition that may be associated with dehydration or diabetes mellitus. A low specific gravity in the polyuria may accompany lithium use

Complete Blood Count (CBC)

The CBC is an another inexpensive test that can reveal considerable data in the initial evaluation of some depressed patients. A complete blood count includes, among other measures:

- The red cell count
- The white cell count
- The hematocrit
- The hemoglobin

Approximately one in five people in the U.S. are anemic. Anemia is often manifested by, among other symptoms:

- Lethargy
- Fatigue
- Malaise

While anemic patients may not appear to be classically depressed, the fatigue and lethargy may be mistaken for symptoms of depression. The incidence of anemia may warrant a CBC in screening most depressed patients, particularly:

- Women of child-bearing years
- Patients over age 65
- Patients with an active alcohol problem

The leukocyte count, or white blood count (WBC), allows screening for infectious etiologies to patients' symptoms and may also provide evidence for serious conditions, such as leukemia. Infectious disorders, from influenza and pneumonia to acquired immunodeficiency syndrome (AIDS), may produce confounding symptoms; the CBC may be the first solid clue to the etiology of these symptoms.

Some drugs used to treat depression also may affect the leukocyte count: lithium is associated with a mild increase in the white count, usually in the range of 12,000 to 16,000; and carbamazepine may be rarely associated with an aplastic anemia. The mean corpuscular volume (MCV) describes the average volume of a red cell, which may be elevated in alcoholism.

While there are no reliable screening tests for alcoholism, an elevated MCV in the context of other abnormalities, such as elevated liver enzymes and gamma glutamyl transferase, may raise the suspicion of occult alcoholism.

Vitamin B_{12} deficiency is also associated with depression and can result in an increased MCV.

An elevated MCV in elderly patients or patients with histories of gastric surgery should be followed by serum B_{12} levels.

Serum Glucose

Abnormalities in glucose metabolism are present in two to eight percent of the population, with diabetes mellitus and hypoglycemia being the two most common disorders. A fasting serum glucose is probably an adequate screening test for these disorders. Urine glucose may only show glucose levels that correlate with serum glucose greater than 200 mg/dl; but glucose levels in the 110 to 200 mg/dl range will be indicated by a fasting serum glucose, which may be associated with lethargy, fatigue, anxiety, and listlessness without associated symptoms of diabetes, such as excessive urination, thirst, and weight loss. Thus, a fasting sugar has significant utility as a screening test for elevated glucose and is more sensitive than a urine dipstick. Hypoglycemia (low blood sugar) is usually associated with early diabetes or the use of hypoglycemic drugs, such as insulin. Recurrent low blood sugars without known cause (idiopathic hypoglycemia) are probably less common than the popular press indicates. Hypoglycemia is associated with symptoms of:

- Anxiety
- Agitation
- Tremulousness
- Irritability

Fasting blood sugars consistently below 50 mg/dl require follow-up studies and referral to an endocrinologist.

Renal Function Tests

Two tests of renal function included in comprehensive chemistry panels are the blood urea nitrogen (BUN) and the serum creatinine, which should probably be obtained in the screening studies of all depressed patients. The kidney clears most antidepressants and lithium, so evidence of kidney damage may indicate an increased risk of toxicity with antidepressants. Furthermore, uremia may manifest as lethargy and apathy; the BUN and creatinine serve as simple measures of renal function. The serum creatinine tends to increase only with extensive kidney damage, while the BUN is more sensitive, may rise with dehydration, and may signal more modest damage.

Serum Electrolytes

Many serum electrolytes can have a significant impact on mental status and may also be influenced by medications used to treat depression. Therefore, obtaining baseline serum electrolytes can be important for depressed patients who:

- Are elderly
- Show acute mental status changes
- Are malnourished
- Take diuretics and/or other medications known to influence electrolytes levels

Several electrolytes may be particularly consequential for depressed patients.

Alterations in serum sodium, such as hyponatremia (low sodium), may manifest with moderately low sodium levels as:

- Irritability
- Depression
- Anxiety

With more pronounced hyponatremia, delirium may be seen and can progress to coma and death. Hyponatremia may be seen in Addison's disease and in various nephropathies. It is occasionally seen in drug therapy and has been reported with use of:

- Lithium
- Carbamazepine
- Fluoxetine (Prozac)

Fluctuations in serum calcium are frequently associated with:

- Weakness
- Asthenia (loss of strength)
- Depression

Both hypocalcemia and hypercalcemia can produce these psychiatric sequelae. Hypocalcemia most commonly results from:

- Vitamin D deficiency
- Nephritis
- Hypoparathyroidism

Hypercalcemia may be associated with:

- Vitamin D intoxication
- Hyperparathyroidism

Potassium levels may be reduced with the temporary emesis and diarrhea associated with antidepressant agents, such as:

- Selective serotonin re-uptake inhibitors (SSRIs)
- Venlafaxine (Effexor)
- Lithium

Low potassium is also occasionally seen when depression results in severe malnutrition. Other common causes of hypokalemia include:

- Cushing's disease
- Diuretic use

Associated with hypokalemia are:

- Weakness
- Apprehension
- Depression
- Lethargy

Both low and high potassium levels may cause arrhythmias. Some antidepressants, particularly the tricyclics, may also induce arrhythmias; and baseline electrolytes as well as EKGs are indicated in patients who begin tricyclic treatment.

Total Protein

The total protein is the sum of the serum proteins. Most antidepressants are tightly bound to the serum proteins, including agents in the two most popular classes – the tricyclics and the selective serotonin re-uptake inhibitors. A protein deficiency may increase the toxicity of antidepressants, since there may be more free drug available to produce adverse reactions. Low protein levels may also be associated with:

- Hepatic disease
- Aging
- The malnutrition sometimes seen in severe depression

The total protein provides a quick assay of nutrition and hydration status.

Hepatic Enzymes

The liver is responsible for the metabolism of all antidepressants except lithium. Hepatic damage may result in greater toxicity when these medications are used. Two enzymes commonly measured as evidence that hepatic damage is in progress are:

- The aspartate aminotransferase (AST, also called the SGOT)
- The alanine aminotransferase (ALT, also called the SGPT)

The AST and ALT do not provide an estimate of liver function efficiency but may suggest current damage. For example, the AST may be more elevated in alcoholic hepatitis, and the ALT may be significantly elevated in patients with drug-induced inflammation or viral hepatitis. Pronounced elevations of one or both enzymes (greater than 500 units per liter) occur with:

- Acute viral injury, including viral hepatitis
- Drug-induced injuries
- Ischemic hepatitis

More modest elevations (less than 300 units per liter) may be seen with:

- Chronic hepatitis
- Cirrhosis
- Biliary obstruction

Several antidepressant drugs have been implicated in elevating hepatic enzymes, including:

- SSRIs, such as fluoxetine (Prozac) and sertraline (Zoloft)
- The tricyclic antidepressants

The clinical significance of this alteration of liver enzymes is unknown and idiosyncratic in occurrence. Thus, routine monitoring of liver enzymes appears to be of little use with patients taking antidepressants.

Valproic acid, on the other hand, is increasingly used to treat some depressive disorders and may rarely produce fulminant hepatic failure. Serious hepatic toxicity with valproate is dose-dependent and tends to occur in the first six months of treatment. Hence, there is a role for monitoring hepatic enzymes with valproate.

Experimental Tests in the Assessment of Depression

Dexamethasone Suppression Test (DST)

The DST is a fairly simple test for disorders of cortisol production, such as Cushing's disease. It has been hypothesized for many years that major depression is related to an abnormality in the hypothalamic pituitary axis (HPA). Some evidence for this is the data that patients with major depression frequently have positive DSTs when they are depressed but not when they are in remission. The fact that depressed patients tend to be non-suppressors of cortisol in the DST lead to hope that DSTs could be used to help confirm the diagnosis of major depression. This hope largely has been unfulfilled because the DST appears to lack both the sensitivity and specificity for useful evaluation of major depression. The specificity is about 90 percent when depressed patients are compared to normal controls but is lower when distinguishing patients with major depression from those with other psychiatric disorders.

DST sensitivity in predicting depression is estimated at only 45 percent.

Given the low specificity and sensitivity of a positive DST in major depression, DSTs should not be used routinely in assessing major depression. A negative DST should not dissuade clinicians from pursuing aggressive antidepressant treatment, and a positive DST does not necessarily indicate the need for somatic therapy. However, the American Psychiatric Association Task Force on the DST and various investigators have proposed several special situations in which DSTs may be somewhat useful:

1. For patients resistant to somatic therapy – Patients with major depression who have a positive DST may be somewhat more receptive to the idea that somatic treatment is indicated if, through DST results, they are presented with data that suggest a biological abnormality. Some data suggest that a positive DST may predict response to somatic treatment, but these results have been inconsistent.

2. For distinguishing between pseudopsychotic symptoms and the dysphoria of a personality disorder, such as borderline personality or psychotic depression – Patients with borderline personality frequently complain of depression and may also describe derogatory voices and paranoid symptoms. The sensitivity of DSTs for psychotic depression appears even greater than for major depression.

Some data also indicate that DST may be elevated in borderline patients with or without major depression. Since treatment of psychotic depression is substantially different from treatment of borderline personality, a strongly positive DST may occasionally push clinicians toward the diagnosis of psychotic depression. Good clinical assessment and judgment, however, are considerably more important than DST results.

3. For predicting relapse – Patients who have an apparent remission of symptoms but continue to produce positive DSTs without medical explanation (such as concurrent anticonvulsant drug use, pregnancy, or Cushing's disease) appear at greater risk for relapse. Clinicians may opt for longer medication trials and monitoring of DSTs for these patients. DSTs that have normalized may indicate relative safety for discontinuing antidepressant treatment.

DST Procedure

1. Baseline cortisol drawn on day one at about 11:00 p.m., followed immediately by one mg dexamethasone orally.
2. Serum cortisols drawn on day two at 8:00 a.m., 4:00 p.m., and 11:00 p.m.

The test is typically considered abnormal if the postdexamethasone cortisol levels are greater than 5 mg/dl.

Thyrotropin-Releasing Hormone Stimulation Test (TRHST)

Thyrotropin-releasing hormone (TRH) from the hypothalamus stimulates the production of thyroid-stimulating hormone (TSH) in the pituitary. The TRHST may be a sensitive test for determining so-called "subclinical hypothyroidism" that may contribute to depressive symptoms. Grade III, or subclinical hypothyroidism, is a controversial diagnosis not accepted by all endocrinologists. In addition, approximately 30 percent of patients with major depression show an abnormal TSH response to the TRHST.

These abnormalities, however, are inconsistent. Some depressed patients have a blunted TSH response to TRH stimulation, while others have an exaggerated TSH response. There is some correlation between a positive TRHST and both the severity of depression and potential for suicide. At this time, these correlations are experimental only, and there appears to be no justification for using the TRHST on a regular basis for depressed patients. However, there may be an occasional depressed patient for whom the TRHST is worth considering.

One such patient is the otherwise euthyroid female over age 50. This population may be at particular risk for hypothyroidism, and the TSH and T_4 may be normal. In Grade III, or subclinical hypothyroidism, the TSH and T_4 serum levels are normal, but the TSH response to TRH is blunted. Patients with a positive TRHST but otherwise normal thyroid function tests may still be candidates for thyroid hormone replacement therapy.

Another patient for whom the TRHST may deserve more consideration is the seriously depressed patient who has not responded to at least two adequate trials of antidepressants. The TRHST may serve two purposes for these patients; it may:

- Possibly detect subclinical hypothyroidism that may be complicating response to treatment
- Provide data about possible augmentation strategies

Cytomel (T_3) and lithium are among the two most common medications used to augment or enhance the effects of standard antidepressants. These agents are sometimes added to a given antidepressant in an attempt to induce more complete response in patients who are partial or nonresponders (see Section #16). An abnormal TRHST may motivate clinicians to consider cytomel augmentation before other strategies. A TRHST baseline may also be of value if lithium is employed as an augmentor, since lithium may induce a hypothyroidism with long-term treatment.

TRHST Procedure

1. A baseline TSH drawn at 9:00 a.m., followed by IV bolus of 500 mg over three minutes.

2. A second TSH drawn at 9:20 a.m.

The TSH should increase by 5 to 25 mIU/ml. Increases in TSH above 30 mIU/ml are associated with hypothyroidism, even in the face of otherwise normal thyroid function tests. Patients with hyperthyroidism tend to have increases of less than 5 mIU/ml.

References:

American Psychiatric Association Task Force on the Use of Laboratory Tests in Psychiatry: The dexamethasone suppression test: An overview of its current status in psychiatry. Am J Psychiatry 1987;144:1253-1262.

Anfinson TJ, Kathol RG: Laboratory and neuroendocrine assessment in medical-psychiatric patients. In: Psychiatric care of the medical patient. Stoudemire A, Fogel BS. Oxford University Press, New York, 1993.

Klee CG, Hay ID: Sensitive thyrotropin assays: Analytic and clinical performance criteria. Mayo Clin Proc 1988;63:1123-1132.

Koran LM, Sox HC, Marton KI et al.: Medical evaluation of psychiatric patients: Results in a state mental health system. Arch Gen Psychiatry 1989;46:733-740.

Loosen PT, Garblutt JC, Prange AJ: Evaluation of diagnostic utility of TRH-induced TSH response in psychiatric disorders. Pharmacopsychiatry 1987;20:90-95.

Nemeroff CB, Evans DL: Correlation between the dexamethasone suppression test in depressed patients and clinical response. Am J Psychiatry 1984;141:247-249.

Rosse RB, Giese AA, Deutsch SI, Morihisa JM: Laboratory diagnostic testing in psychiatry. APA Press, Washington, 1989.

Targum SD, Greenberg R, Harmoin RL et al.: Thyroid hormone and the TRH stimulation test in refractory depression. J Clinical Psychiatry 1984;45:345-346.

#4 Antidepressant Medications

There are a growing number of treatment options for major depression, and choosing the appropriate treatment can be a daunting task. The choices include:

- Medications
- Electroconvulsive therapy
- Various forms of psychotherapy
- Combinations of the above

4. Approximately two dozen antidepressant medications are on the market, and the number is increasing every year. The newer antidepressants, especially fluoxetine (Prozac), have been among the most financially successful medications ever developed. Its success has garnered abundant publicity about the medication, both good and bad. According to the lay press, the newer antidepressants are either miracle drugs or a significant public health hazard, and recent best-selling books, such as Peter Kramer's *Listening to Prozac*, have done much to spark public interest and debate about antidepressants.

Millions of prescriptions are written every year for antidepressants, approximately 80 percent by primary care physicians. Clearly, not all these prescriptions are needed or are necessarily in the best interests of patients. Some patients receive antidepressant drugs even when the diagnosis of major depression seems unlikely, but many who could benefit from antidepressants are not getting them. The following guidelines may help clinicians formulate a treatment approach after a diagnosis of major depression is established.

The Need for Drug Therapy

The decision to pursue treatment of major depressive episode with medications may be a difficult one. All antidepressants have physical side effects that must be weighed against the potential benefits of treatment. Also to be considered are the "halo" effect (i.e., some patients, who clearly could benefit from these medications, refuse them because of their identification as "psychiatric" drugs and the stigma attached to taking them) and the fact that some depressive episodes may be effectively treated without antidepressants.

There is good clinical consensus that certain features of a major depressive episode tip the risk-to-benefit scale in favor of antidepressant medications. The first feature of these has to do with severity of illness.

Major depression varies in severity but is usually:

- Painful
- Disabling
- Often life-threatening

As a rule, the more severe the depression, the more an antidepressant trial is warranted. Patients with more severe vegetative symptoms, such as weight loss of more than 10 percent of body weight in one month and unrelenting insomnia, are also good candidates for drug treatment.

A second feature of depression that indicates the need for an antidepressant trial is significant impairment in social and occupational functioning. Some patients lose the ability to work and become so withdrawn that they refuse any contact with the outside world. Such patients may become emotionally unavailable to family members and isolate themselves from loved ones. A vicious cycle ensues wherein patients' isolation exacerbates depression; and, in their depressed and withdrawn states, they feel even more hopeless and disconnected and isolate themselves further. Antidepressants may stop this cycle and facilitate a general improvement in function.

Patients at significant risk for suicide may frequently be saved by intensive treatment, including use of antidepressant drugs; for patients who are suicidal secondary to a major depression, antidepressants may treat the underlying depression and mitigate the risk. However, some older classes of antidepressants (e.g., the tricyclics) are potentially lethal in overdose and require careful monitoring.

Major depression is usually a recurring illness. Many studies indicate that continued use of antidepressants substantially reduces the risk of recurrence (see Section #16). Thus, patients with histories of multiple serious depressive episodes should be considered for long-term antidepressant treatment. Common guidelines for determining candidates for long-term treatment are:

- If patients have experienced two or more severe depressive episodes in the past five years
- If patients have experienced more than three severe depressive episodes in a lifetime

Some subtypes of major depression do not appear to be responsive to psychotherapy and frequently require more aggressive treatment. For example, melancholic, psychotic, and bipolar depression (see Section #15) usually do not appear amenable to psychotherapy alone. A combination of medication and electroconvulsive therapy may be effective treatment options for these subtypes.

Obviously, patients with good past response to antidepressant treatment are reasonable candidates for resumption of antidepressant medications. Good past response to antidepressants usually, but not always, predicts good future response to drug therapy.

Finally, it is not unusual in today's culture for patients to walk into clinics and request specific antidepressants. Given the massive publicity that drugs such as fluoxetine (Prozac) have received in the lay press, this interest is to be expected. If patients meet criteria for major depression and no specific contraindications exist, it may be reasonable to honor these requests.

Unfortunately, many patients who are not clinically depressed also hope to feel or function better by taking such medications. While many nondepressed patients claim to feel better on antidepressants, there is no scientific evidence for employing antidepressants in this population. Employing antidepressants in patients who have no clear indications for taking them constitutes drug abuse and should be discouraged.

Overview of the Antidepressant Drugs

Antidepressant drugs are a chemically heterogeneous group of compounds. They include:

- Cyclic antidepressants (tricyclic and tetracyclics)
- Monoamine oxidase inhibitors (MAOIs)
- Serotonin re-uptake inhibitors (SSRIs)
- Serotonin norepinephrine re-uptake inhibitors
- 5-HT_2 antagonists
- Other agents

Although these antidepressant drugs differ considerably in chemical structure and effects, they share a number of common properties. All the available antidepressants seem to work by influencing certain neurotransmitters in the brain, including:

- Serotonin
- Norepinephrine
- Dopamine

These three monoamine neurotransmitters are chemically related; neurotransmitters form a basis for chemical communication between and among nerve cells in the brain. All neurotransmitters work by facilitating or inhibiting electrical impulses across the space, or synapse, between neighboring neurons. An important theory on the cause of depression is the monoamine hypothesis, which states that major depression is caused by a deficiency of monoamine neurotransmitters in certain parts of the brain or, possibly, in the function the monoamine receptors. This deficiency could result from a number of factors, including:

- A genetic predisposition to the deficiency state
- Psychological stress
- A secondary effect of taking certain medications

In fact, the monoamine hypothesis is based on evidence that drugs that deplete monoamines, such as reserpine, are implicated in causing depression.

On the other hand, antidepressants tend to enhance monoamine neurotransmission. There are some problems with the monoamine hypothesis of depression; these problems suggest the issue is far more complicated and is beyond the scope of this discussion. However, it is clear that current antidepressants have potent effects on the monoamine system.

Antidepressants can increase the availability of monoamine neurotransmitters in the synaptic clefts of the brain by several means. However, the antidepressants largely employ two methods to enhance brain monoamines; they are:

- Blocking the re-uptake of monoamine neurotransmitters
- Blocking the breakdown of neurotransmitters

Re-uptake is one of the ways the brain recycles neurotransmitters (see Figure 4.1). In method one, antidepressants, such as cyclic

FIGURE 4.1 – **The Effect of Antidepressants on Neurotransmitters**

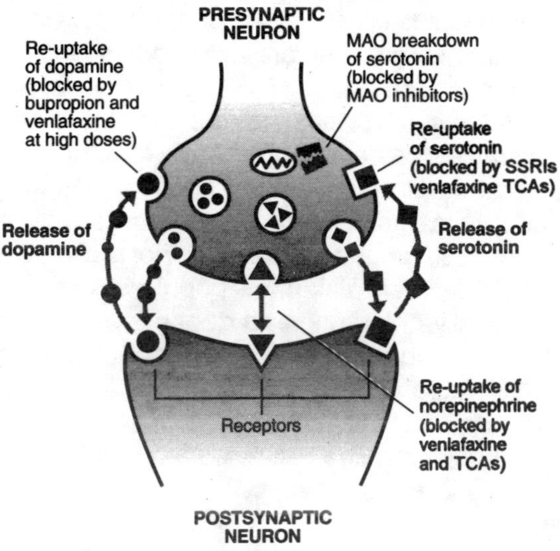

agents and SSRIs, increase the time spent by the monoamine neurotransmitters in the synaptic cleft by blocking re-uptake of the neurotransmitters. Thus, the availability of monoamine neurotransmitters is enhanced and communication is facilitated between and among neurons.

In method two, antidepressants act on the monoamine system by blocking the breakdown of the neurotransmitters. Monoamine oxidase is one of the primary enzymes responsible for the breakdown of monoamine neurotransmitters in neurons and others cells. The MAOIs prevent the breakdown of monoamine neurotransmitters, thereby increasing the availability of monoamines in the synaptic cleft.

There are other methods by which antidepressants may work, but these two may account for much of the efficacy of antidepressants.

Another property of all prescription antidepressants is that they are not "addictive" in the usual sense of the word. This is an important point for patients who may equate mood-elevating agents, such as antidepressants, to illicit drugs, such as amphetamines and cocaine. Although antidepressants and some illicit drugs may enhance mood, antidepressants do not produce the "buzz" that would make them popular street drugs. Additionally, tolerance and dependence are not features of long-term antidepressant use. Occasionally, mild withdrawal symptoms are associated with rapid discontinuance of some antidepressants, but these instances are relatively rare and are more of a nuisance than a serious problem.

An unfortunate feature of all antidepressants is that they typically take time to begin working. It is not unusual for three weeks to pass before patients report any relief from their symptoms, and full antidepressant effects may not be evident for two months or more. Thus, an antidepressant trial of less than four to six weeks is probably not adequate to determine efficacy. Patients should be reassured that it will take time for their antidepressant medications to take effect, though they may complain of side effects from the first day of the trial. Many side effects, however, disappear after four to eight weeks of treatment.

Though there is some variability from patient to patient, a common sequence of improvement generally occurs with antidepressant therapy. Improvements in sleep and ease of anxiety are often evident in the first week, and minor improvements in motivation and interest, hopefulness, and appetite are frequently evident by the second and third weeks of treatment. Mood and libido are usually among the last symptoms to improve.

Commonly, patients' family members are aware of improvements before patients are. Improvements are gradual and steady in most patients; some patients report waking up one morning, usually after several weeks of treatment, and finally feeling better.

Antidepressants generally share the same rate of efficacy. For any given depressive episode, about 60 to 70 percent of patients respond to a single trial, regardless of which antidepressant is used. The exception occurs in patients having certain subtypes of depression who may respond preferentially to certain agents (see Section #15).

Overall, approximately 90 percent of patients eventually respond to drug treatment, though several different trials and combinations of drugs may be tried before optimal response is seen. However, response does not necessarily result in complete remission of symptoms. Many patients with substantial improvements experience some residual symptoms that may last for months, despite adequate pharmacotherapy.

Choosing an Antidepressant

Clinicians are faced with a wide variety of choices in antidepressant treatment, and choosing the proper medication for a specific patient may sometimes be as much an art as it is a science. Because it is generally equal for all antidepressants, efficacy is usually not a major variable in choosing medications. Patient and drug parameters ultimately determine optimal selections of antidepressant therapy.

Drug parameters include:

- Side effect profile
- Safety in overdose
- Activating versus sedating properties
- Cost

The side effect profile is perhaps the most important factor. In contrast to efficacy, the side effect profile differs dramatically from class to class. The success of the newer antidepressants stems greatly from their superior side effect profile as compared to cyclic antidepressants and MAOIs. SSRIs, such as fluoxetine (Prozac), are among the best tolerated, are relatively safe in overdose, and thus are the most common first-line antidepressants used (see Table 4.1). Likewise, newer agents, such as venlafaxine (Effexor), bupropion (Wellbutrin), and the serotonin antagonists,

TABLE 4.1 — **Choosing an Antidepressant by Side Effect Profile, Safety and Ease of Use**

FIRST-LINE AGENTS	SECOND-LINE AGENTS
Selective Serotonin Re-uptake Inhibitors	*Secondary Amine Tricyclics*
Fluoxetine (Prozac)	Desipramine (Norpramin)
Fluvoxamine (Luvox)	Nortriptyline (Pamelor)
Paroxetine (Paxil)	Other Cyclic Antidepressants
Sertraline (Zoloft)	
Selective Serotonin/Norepinephrine Re-uptake Inhibitors	**THIRD-LINE AGENTS**
Venlafaxine (Effexor)	
5-HT_2 Antagonists	*Monoamine Oxidase Inhibitors*
Nefazodone (Serzone)	Tranylcypromine (Parnate)
Trazodone (Desyrel)	Phenelzine (Nardil)
Atypical Antidepressant	
Bupropion (Wellbutrin)	

trazodone and nefazodone, share a favorable side effect profile and appear relatively safe in overdose.

Second-line agents, by safety and side effect profile, include the cyclic antidepressants. While the secondary amine tricyclic drugs, such as nortriptyline (Pamelor) and desipramine (Norpramin), are typically the best tolerated drugs in the class, all cyclic drugs have more noticeable side effects than first-line agents. However, some patients have no problems with cyclic antidepressants but cannot tolerate one day's treatment on SSRIs. Another significant disadvantage of cyclic antidepressants is their potential to be fatal in overdose. Suicide attempts are common in depressed patients; an overdose with the equivalent of 1500 mg of imipramine may prove lethal in many patients.

The MAOIs have been relegated to third-line status by virtue of:

- Dietary restrictions required during the trial
- Their potential for lethal drug interactions
- Their frequent side effects

Nonetheless, these are important medications that are still commonly used.

Some antidepressants, such as fluoxetine (Prozac), the secondary amine tricyclics (nortriptyline [Pamelor] and desipramine [Norpramin]), bupropion (Wellbutrin), and the MAOIs are experienced as more "activating" than others; but it is unclear if this tendency is related to a proclivity of some medications to produce treatment emergent restlessness and agitation. However, some antidepressants are clearly less sedating than others and may be useful in patients with more "retarded" depressions who also suffer from hypersomnia. During initiation of treatment, activating antidepressants may be more poorly tolerated in patients with prominent agitation, anxiety, and insomnia. In the long-run, however, activating antidepressants are just as effective in patients with agitated depression. The more sedating antidepressants include:

- Trazodone (Desyrel)
- The tertiary amine tricyclics, such as amitriptyline (Elavil) and imipramine (Tofranil)

Medication cost is often a crucial factor in the selection of an antidepressant. The older classes of antidepressants are less expensive because their patents have expired and they are available in generic formulations. The generic forms of tricyclics and MAOIs generally cost less than $10.00 for a month's supply (see Table 4.2).

By contrast, a month's supply of SSRIs can cost four to six times that amount. Nonetheless, advantages of the newer agents generally appear to justify the costs.

Patient parameters in drug selection include:

- Age
- Weight
- Gender
- Medical status

Age is one of the most important patient parameters in the choice of antidepressants. Hepatic metabolism and renal clearance is typically reduced in the elderly; these conditions may result in greater sensitivity to the toxic effects of some medications. Doses typically need to be reduced in these patients. Some antidepressants are poorly tolerated by the elderly even at small doses and should be avoided if possible. Among the greatest offenders are the anticholinergic tricyclic drugs, such as amitriptyline (Elavil); these drugs may present a large anticholinergic load at relatively small doses and produce more mischief than benefit. The first-line agents tend to be the favored agents in the treatment of geriatric depression (see Section #14).

Though antidepressants are not typically dosed according to body mass, weight may be an important issue in their dosing schedule. Many other medications, including anticonvulsants, are dosed according to body mass; and, since tricyclic antidepressants have chemical structures and properties similar to some anticonvulsants such as carbamazepine (Tegretol), it is conceivable that the optimal dose of some antidepressants may need to be determined accordingly. The optimal dose may be different, for example, for a 95-pound female than for a 340-pound male. Furthermore, the weight gain associated with some antidepressants may be particularly problematic for some patients. In patients concerned about weight gain, it is generally a good idea to avoid the antidepressants more strongly associated with weight gain. These include:

- MAOIs
- Lithium
- Certain tricyclic drugs, such as:
  - Amitriptyline (Elavil)
  - Doxepin (Sinequan)
  - Imipramine (Tofranil)

SSRIs and bupropion (Wellbutrin), however, may have a mild anorectic effect.

Gender is rarely an issue in the choice of optimal antidepressants except as it affects other parameters, such as medical status. Many antidepressants adversely affect sexual function in men and women, the most common offenders being MAOIs and SSRIs. Less problematic in compromising sexual function are:

- Bupropion (Wellbutrin)
- Trazodone (Desyrel)
- Nefazodone (Serzone)

Trazodone (Desyrel), however, is associated with the rare occurrence of priapism in men and must be monitored in young male patients.

Patients' medical status is extremely important in antidepressant selection. Generally, patients in poor medical health may tolerate first-line agents (see Table 4.1) better than other antidepressants, though some medical conditions contraindicate antidepressant use. Patients with seizure disorders, for example, should not be treated with bupropion (Wellbutrin), which may induce seizures at high doses in susceptible patients. Similarly, elderly patients and those with postural hypotension may be at risk for falls with the use of trazodone (Desyrel) because of its tendency to produce orthostatic drops in blood pressure. Venlafaxine (Effexor) has the opposite effect and may increase blood pressure at higher doses; thus, patients who take this drug and have pre-existing severe hypertension and cardiovascular status such that small sustained increases in blood pressure are problematic (i.e., end-stage congestive heart failure) must be monitored.

SSRIs, especially fluoxetine (Prozac) and paroxetine (Paxil), are associated with increasing serum levels and toxicity when used concurrently with some drugs, including certain antiarrythmia drugs and tricyclics. Such potential interactions require monitoring but do not necessarily contraindicate use of these drugs in patients also taking cardiovascular drugs.

Matching antidepressants to patients requires attention to both drug and patient parameters. These parameters should be reviewed and antidepressants chosen accordingly.

Duration of Treatment

Given that maximum benefits of antidepressant therapy are often not seen for four to eight weeks, shorter trials appear to be inadequate, especially when four to eight weeks is required for therapeutic doses to be achieved. In this case, at least four weeks of therapy at the optimum dose is required before considering discontinuance of therapy. For example, since the therapeutic dose of imipramine (Tofranil) is typically in the 150- to 300-mg per day dose range, the two weeks or longer required to achieve this range should not be included as part of the therapy trial period. An adequate trial of imipramine is four or more weeks at the 150- to 300-mg per day dose range. It is probably reasonable to discontinue an antidepressant if there is absolutely no improvement at four weeks at therapeutic doses. However, patients with partial response may continue to improve over the next eight weeks.

If partial or complete remission of the major depressive episode is achieved, clinical consensus indicates that the trial should be continued for at least six months. Discontinuing the medication before that time appears to increase the risk of relapse greatly. This may be analogous to the use of a cast to mend a broken bone; it takes a number of weeks for a broken bone to heal, and removing a cast too early will result in inadequate bone repair. On the other hand, wearing a cast beyond the optimum period is of no benefit. Currently, there is no clear evidence that continuing an antidepressant for longer than six months is useful to patients who have experienced a single major depressive episode. Patients with multiple, severe recurrences of major depression, however, appear to benefit from long-term, even lifetime treatment with antidepressants (see Section #15).

References:

Baldessarini RJ: Chemotherapy in psychiatry. Harvard University Press, Cambridge, 1986.

Cole JO, Bodkin JAA: Antidepressant drug side effects. J Clin Psychiatry 1990;51(suppl 1):21-26.

Lin EH, Von Korff M, Katon W et al: The role of the primary care physician in patients' adherence to antidepressant therapy. Med Care 1995;33:67-74.

Murphy DL, Campbell I, Costa JL: Current status of the indolamine hypothesis of the affective disorders. In: Psychopharmacology: A generation of progress. Lipton MA, DiMascio A, Killam KF. Raven Press, New York, 1978.

Nierenberg AA: The medical consequences of the selection of an antidepressant. J Clin Psychiatry 1992;53:19-24.

Paykel ES: Management of acute depression. In: Psychopharmacology of affective disorders. Paykel ES, Coppen A. Oxford University Press, New York, 1979.

Price LH, Charney DS, Delgado PL et al: Clinical data on the role of serotonin in the mechanism(s) of action of antidepressant drugs. J Clin Psychiatry 1990;51:44-50; discussion 51-52.

Quitkin FM, Rabkin JG, Ross D et al.: Duration of antidepressant drug treatment: What is an adequate trial? Arch Gen Psychiatry 1984;41:238-245.

Richelson E: Synaptic pharmacology of antidepressants: An update. McClean Hosp J 1988; 13:67-88.

Simon GE, Von Korff M, Wagner EH et al: Patterns of antidepressant use in community practice. Gen Hosp Psychiatry 1993;15:399-408.

Tollefson GD: Adverse drug reactions/interactions in maintenance therapy. J Clin Psychiatry 1993;54:48-58; discussion 59-60.

Tollefson GD, Holman SL: How long to onset of antidepressant action: A meta-analysis of patients treated with fluoxetine or placebo. Int Clin Psychopharmacol 1994;9:245-250.

TABLE 4.2 – Strengths and Costs per 100 Pills of Antidepressant Drugs

Drug	Strength (mg)	Cost per 100 units*	Therapeutic Dose/day	Monthly Cost**
Antidepressants				
TCAs				
Amitriptyline (Elavil)	25	$3.00	150 mg	$5.40
Amoxapine (Asendin)	25	53.00	150 mg	95.40
Clomipramine (Anatrinil)	50	106.00	150 mg	95.40
Desipramine (Norpramin)	25	24.00	150 mg	43.20
Doxepin (Sinegan)	25	13.00	150 mg	23.40
Imipramine (Tofranil)	25	4.00	150 mg	7.20
Maprotiline (Ludiomil)	25	28.00	150 mg	45.00
Nortriptyline (Pamelor)	25	70.00	50 mg	42.00
Protriptyline (Vivactil)	10	66.00	15 mg	29.70
Trimipramine (Surmontil)	25	63.00	150 mg	133.40
SSRI				
Fluoxetine (Prozac)	20	228.02	20 mg	68.67
Paroxetine (Paxil)	20	201.55	20 mg	60.47
Sertraline (Zoloft)	100	209.28	50 mg	34.88
Fluvoxamine (Luvox)	100	196.51	100 mg	58.96
Other				
Venlafaxine (Effexor)	75	107.34	75 mg	32.20
5HT-2				
Trazodone (Trazodone)	150	70.35	300 mg	42.21
Nefazodone (Serzone)	150	72.63	300 mg	43.58
MAOI				
Phenelzine (Nardil)	15	38.00	15 mg	11.40
Tranylcypromine (Parnate)	10	44.00	10 mg	13.20
Atypical				
Bupropion (Wellbutrin)	100	75.11	300 mg	67.50

* Cost is reported as the average wholesale price (AWP) based on the 1996 Redbook.

** Monthly cost based on tablet strength listed for each drug. Actual monthly cost may be substantially lower since higher strength tablets may be available at proportionally lower cost. Costs also may vary from pharmacy to pharmacy.

(Adapted from Schatzberg AF, Cole JO, DeBattista C: Manual of Clinical Psychopharmacology, Third Edition, APA Press, Washington DC, 1996.)

#5 Selective Serotonin Re-uptake Inhibitors

In the seven years since fluoxetine (Prozac) was introduced, the selective serotonin re-uptake inhibitors (SSRIs) have emerged as the most popular antidepressants of all time.

These are a chemically diverse group of drugs that also include paroxetine (Paxil) and sertraline (Zoloft). In addition, fluvoxamine (Luvox) was released in 1995. Fluvoxamine is FDA approved only for use in obsessive compulsive disorder (OCD). However, numerous studies have suggested that fluvoxamine also may have a role to play in the treatment of depression.

5. This class of medications is the product of research performed in the late 1960s and 1970s that sought selective properties as a way of reducing the side effects associated with non-selective antidepressants, such as cyclic drugs and monoamine oxidase inhibitors. The effort was successful; SSRIs are generally better tolerated than the older agents and appear to be of equal efficacy. They also are relatively safe in overdose and are easy to use.

Mechanism of Action

SSRIs, as suggested by the name, block the re-uptake of serotonin in the central nervous system. The blockage increases the amount of serotonin available to the postsynaptic neuron and may correct the supposed monoamine deficiency state associated with depression. However, though re-uptake effects are immediate, maximum clinical effects are not seen for weeks. A

TABLE 5.1 — **The Selective Serotonin Re-uptake Inhibitors (SSRIs)**

Agent	Advantages	Disadvantages	Dose
Fluoxetine (Prozac)	Best studied SSRI Positive press	Activating properties Negative press	20 – 60 mg/day
Fluvoxamine (Luvox)	Low IID_6 inhibition	Split dosing High $IIIA_{3/4}$ inhibitor	100 – 300 mg/day
Paroxetine (Paxil)	Most potent SSRI in serotonin re-uptake Easy dosing	Most anticholinergic SSRI	20 – 50 mg/day
Sertraline (Zoloft)	Only SSRI with clear dose-response curve	Large dose range	50 – 200 mg/day

change in sensitivity in the 5-HT (serotonin) and frequently in the central adrenergic receptors is seen with repeated administration of SSRIs; thus, chronic administration of this and other antidepressants is associated with a change in receptors that may be important to clinical antidepressant response.

Relative selectivity of SSRIs suggests that these drugs do not significantly affect other transmitter systems that produce adverse effects associated with other antidepressants. For example, SSRIs are not particularly antihistaminic; thus, they do not tend to be particularly sedating and are not associated with weight gain. Also, there are virtually no anticholinergic effects, such as dry mouth, constipation, and urinary retention, that occur with cyclic antidepressants; and SSRIs do not block alpha-adrenergic receptors associated with hypotension.

Indications

Most of the many efficacy studies of SSRIs for treatment of depression have focused on outpatients with mild to moderate depression. Clear and convincing data support the use of SSRIs in outpatient treatment of depression, and a few studies also suggest that SSRIs are useful in the treatment of both dysthymia and more serious major depressions that include psychotic and melancholic features. Some investigators suggest that SSRIs may not be the best choice for treatment of more serious depressions and that they may be less effective than other available agents. Currently, only a few studies are investigating the use of SSRIs in serious major depression. Given their favorable features, SSRIs may be considered first-line agents for all subtypes of major depression until data prove otherwise.

SSRIs have proven to be useful in the treatment of other psychiatric disorders, including obsessive compulsive disorder. It is not uncommon for patients with major depression to present with obsessive features, and SSRIs may be a particularly good choice for these patients.

Panic disorder also has been shown to respond to SSRI treatment. Studies have demonstrated antipanic features for most of the SSRIs, though these effects are sometimes seen late in therapy (after six weeks). Higher doses of SSRIs are sometimes required to treat panic. For example, Paxil is FDA approved for the treatment of panic but appears effective in doses of 40 mg per day or more. Anecdotally, fluoxetine (Prozac) may be less well tolerated in the early treatment stages of panic patients because of its somewhat activating properties. With continued use, however, patients seem to adapt to the activating effects and good antipanic results are frequently seen.

Eating disorders, such as bulimia, are reported to be partially responsive to SSRI treatment. There are also growing data that SSRIs are useful in the treatment of premenstrual dysphoria.

There are limited data that suggest SSRIs may help with some addictive behaviors, including alcoholism, but the positive effects have been modest. SSRIs should not be used to treat substance abuse disorders unless a concurrent depressive disorder exists.

Chronic fatigue syndrome anecdotally is said frequently to respond to fluoxetine (Prozac) and other SSRI treatment, but often the chronic fatigue syndrome is linked to associated major depression. There is the rare patient, however, who meets the criteria for chronic fatigue syndrome without significant associated psychiatric co-morbidity and whose condition responds to antidepressant treatment. Chronic fatigue syndrome remains a controversial diagnosis that awaits further study for validation.

SSRIs also have been used to treat chronic pain conditions, such as peripheral neuropathy, fibromyalgia, and some recurrent headaches, with variable success. In addition to influencing the modulation of pain pathways, SSRIs may have a more direct, though modest, analgesic effect.

Since SSRIs appear to be relatively benign agents, patients have been tempted to take them even if a major depression or other clear disorder has not been diagnosed. Indiscriminate use of these or any antidepressants constitutes drug abuse. Certainly, there are anecdotal reports of non-depressed patients with minimal symptoms who report better functioning and being happier on SSRIs. Furthermore, there are anecdotal reports of introverted and timid people becoming more extroverted and assertive. No clear data suggest that SSRIs benefit "the worried well," and there are some side effects associated with their use. Thus, it is prudent that drugs be prescribed only when there is a clear indication for their use.

Side Effects and Their Management

The immense popularity of SSRIs is due greatly to their favorable side effect profile relative to older antidepressants. However, some patients simply cannot tolerate even minuscule doses of any agent in this class. Though side effects vary somewhat among various SSRIs, these drugs share a number of adverse effects.

TABLE 5.2 — Common Side Effects of the Selective Serotonin Re-uptake Inhibitors (SSRIs)

Gastrointestinal Upset	Nausea Diarrhea/Cramping Upset Stomach	
Central Nervous System Activation	Agitation Anxiety	Insomnia Restlessness
Sexual Dysfunction	Anorgasmia Decreased libido Delayed ejaculation	
Other	Dry mouth Headaches	Excessive sweating Tremor

The most common adverse effect reported with SSRIs is gastrointestinal (GI) upset. Approximately 25 to 33 percent of patients taking SSRIs experience some nausea, emesis, diarrhea, cramping, and/or general GI discomfort. These effects are the most common reasons given for patients' discontinuance of treatment. Sertraline (Zoloft) and fluvoxamine (Luvox) seem to produce greater GI difficulties than other SSRIs, but the differences are slight. Adaptation to the GI upset often occurs in the first few weeks of therapy and therefore tends to be a problem primarily in the first two weeks of treatment. If GI upset is evident, the problem may be mitigated by using certain strategies, including:

- Instructing patients to take the medications with food
- Lowering the dose and titrating the dose upwards slowly to allow the body time to adapt to the medication
- In the first few weeks of treatment, adding an antiemetic, antacid, or diarrhea medication for symptomatic treatment
- Reassuring patients that GI upset is common and temporary

Symptoms of central nervous system overarousal, such as insomnia and nervousness, are commonly reported with SSRIs, particularly fluoxetine. Approximately 10 to 20 percent of patients taking SSRIs complain of feeling overstimulated, anxious, and restless. In addition, insomnia can be a problem for some patients. The restlessness associated with SSRI use is similar to that experienced with use of antipsychotic drugs, such as haloperidol, and may, in fact, be related. Some adaptation occurs with the activating effects, but this may take many weeks. Conservative use of anti-anxiety medication, such as lorazepam (Ativan 0.5 mg twice a day) or diazepam (Valium 5 mg twice a day), often helps counteract the arousing effect of SSRIs in the first few weeks of treatment. Frequently, patients who have difficulty falling asleep benefit from taking their medications earlier in the day. To counteract insomnia, fluoxetine (Prozac) should be given in the morning rather than at bedtime. Also, trazodone (Desyrel) 25 to 75 mg at night has been used with considerable success to counteract the insomnia associated with SSRIs.

Conversely, a smaller percentage of patients complain of feeling fatigued, sedated, and somnolent on SSRIs. For these patients, reducing the dose initially and gradually increasing it to optimum levels sometimes helps, as may taking the medication closer to bedtime.

The incidence of sexual dysfunction with use of SSRIs has probably been under-reported. Premarketing studies of fluoxetine (Prozac) suggested that only two percent of patients suffered from such problems as delayed ejaculation and anorgasmia. However, more recent estimates put the incidence of treatment-emergent sexual dysfunction as high as 40 percent. While few people discontinue treatment because of sexual difficulties, the situation is worrisome for many patients. There are anecdotal reports that buspirone (Buspar) in a dose of 30 mg per day or cyproheptadine in doses of 4 to 8 mg per day counteract some sexual side effects of SSRIs. Also, some patients report that holding the dose of shorter-acting SSRIs, such as paroxetine (Paxil) and sertraline (Zoloft), for a day or two before anticipated sexual activity seems to help. Of course, missing too many doses of medications may detract from their efficacy; this option is not recommended.

Some clinicians have also reported the use of amantadine and bupropion in addition to the SSRIs helps the sexual dysfunction. However, SSRIs could conceivably increase bupropion levels and should be used with caution.

Many other side effects may occur with SSRI treatment, including:

- Tremor
- Excessive perspiration
- Rash
- Headache

Though they are annoying to patients, rarely do these side effects lead to discontinuance of treatment.

Contrary to what is written about fluoxetine (Prozac) and other SSRIs in the lay press, there is no convincing scientific evidence that these drugs cause patients to become violent, suicidal, or sexually promiscuous.

Drug Interactions

Though serious drug interactions with SSRIs are relatively rare, two types deserve special attention. The most serious potential drug interaction occurs when SSRIs and monoamine oxidase inhibitors (MAOIs) are used in combination. The combination has resulted in several fatalities, especially with highly serotonergic agents such as clomipramine (Anafranil).

This toxic combination may manifest with symptoms of:

- Mental status changes (e.g., confusion, delirium, and coma)
- Motor abnormalities (e.g., tremor, hypertonia, ataxia, and myoclonus)
- Autonomic dysregulation (diaphoresis and hyperthermia)

These symptoms are consistent with what is sometimes called a "serotonergic syndrome," thought to be caused by an excess of serotonergic activity. Not only is the combination of SSRIs and MAOIs contraindicated, but SSRIs must be discontinued for a period of time before treatment with MAOIs is initiated. Fluoxetine (Prozac) has a particularly long half-life and must be discontinued five weeks prior to starting MAOI treatment; other SSRIs require about two weeks' discontinuance before MAOI treatment is begun.

Another potentially serious drug interaction may occur when SSRIs are used concurrently with drugs that are metabolized by a particular liver enzyme. All SSRIs are capable of inhibiting the IID_6 isoenzyme of the cytochrome P_{450} system responsible for metabolizing the tricyclic antidepressants, carbamazepine (Tegretol), some beta-blockers (metoprolol), certain anti-arrhythmia medications (flecainide and encainide), and many antipsychotic drugs, such thioridazine (Mellaril) and clozapine (Clozaril). When the IID_6 enzyme is inhibited because of the concurrent use of an SSRI, serum levels of drugs dependent on this enzyme rise and serious toxicity may ensue. There are reports of tricyclic levels rising up to eight times their baseline levels and serious arrhythmias being produced when SSRIs are involved.

Paroxetine (Paxil) may be the most potent inhibitor of the IID_6 (see Table 5.3), and fluvoxamine

TABLE 5.3 — Inhibition Constants (Ki) for the Inhibition of Hepatic Enzymes by the Available SSRIs

Smaller Kis are associated with a greater inhibition and a higher potential for interaction with drugs dependent on the IID_6 isoenzyme as well as other cytochrome P_{450} enzymes.

SSRI	Ki
Paroxetine (Paxil)	.15
Fluoxetine (Prozac)	.60
Sertraline (Zoloft)	.70
Fluvoxamine (Luvox)	8.20

Adapted from Crewe HK, 1993.

(Luvox) may be the least potent inhibitor of IID_6; but all SSRIs are capable of causing some problems when used in combination with the drugs mentioned. Fluvoxamine (Luvox) appears to be a potent inhibitor of other enzymes, including the IA_2 and $IIIA_{3/4}$. These enzymes are responsible for the metabolism of such common drugs as caffeine, some benzodiazepines, and terfenadine. Being aware of potential interactions and adjusting dosages of concurrent medications downwards should prevent serious problems.

Dosing

Simple, once-a-day dosing is one of the attractive features of SSRIs. Finding an adequate dose is fairly straightforward for most SSRIs, since the dose-response curve is fairly flat. Most patients, for example, respond to the usual starting dose of fluoxetine (Prozac) of 20 mg per day, and some who do not respond to doses in the 40-mg range. However, many patients do less well at an increased dose of 60 mg per day than at lower doses because of increased side effects. There is no evidence that doses higher than 60 mg per day are useful in the treatment of depression, and substantial evidence that higher doses are more toxic. Thus, a useful strategy is to initiate treatment at 20 mg per day and drop the dosage to 10 mg or lower per day if patients cannot tolerate the initial dosage. Patients who cannot tolerate a 10 mg per day capsule may initiate therapy at 2 mg via a fluoxetine elixir. Fluoxetine (Prozac) is the only SSRI currently available in liquid form. If patients do not respond or respond inadequately after three weeks to a 20 mg per day dose, the dose may be increased as tolerated by 20 mg every two weeks until a maximum daily dose of 60 mg per day is achieved.

Dosing for paroxetine (Paxil) is similar to that of fluoxetine (Prozac), though its studies have been for a maximum dose of only 50 mg per day. Some studies have suggested that more serious depressive episodes may respond to maximum doses of paroxetine.

Sertraline (Zoloft) appears to be an exception to the flat-dose response curve typical of other SSRIs; higher doses are linearly related to response. Most patients respond to a starting dose of 50 mg per day but halve this if the initial dose is poorly tolerated. If patients do not respond or respond inadequately after two weeks to the initial dose, it may be doubled to 100 mg per day, gradually titrating the dose over two weeks' time.

Fluvoxamine (Luvox) was released to the American market in 1995. The usual starting dose is 50 mg per day and may be increased by 50-mg increments every week or two as tolerated. Most patients appear to respond to doses in the 100 to 200 mg per day range; however, some patients appear to require doses up to 300 mg per day. Doses higher than 100 mg per day should be administered in two divided daily doses.

Drug Discontinuance

While SSRIs were initially thought to be free of such withdrawal syndromes, it is clear that rapid discontinuance may be occasionally associated with mild withdrawal symptoms, including:

- Fatigue
- Nausea
- Headaches
- Malaise
- Dizziness

There is speculation that the long half-life of fluoxetine (Prozac) lessens the likelihood of withdrawal symptoms when the drug is rapidly discontinued and that paroxetine (Paxil) may be more associated with withdrawal symptoms because of its more anticholinergic properties and shorter half-life, but little data exist to support either contention. Though the incidence and intensity of withdrawal symptoms associated with SSRIs are low, it is reasonable to taper dosages rather than to stop drug treatment suddenly. There are no guidelines for tapering dosages, but a common strategy is to decrease dosages in weekly increments over two to four weeks. The majority of patients appear to tolerate sudden discontinuance of SSRI treatment without significant complaints.

References:

Cole JO: New directions in antidepressant therapy: A review of sertraline: A unique serotonin re-uptake inhibitor. J Clin Psychiatry 1992;53(9):333-340.

Crewe HK, Lennard MS, Tucker GT et al.: The effect of selective serotonin re-uptake inhibitors on the cytochrome $P4502D_6$ (CYP_2D_6) activity in human liver microsomes. Br J Clin Pharmacol 1992;34:262-265.

DeBattista C, Schatzberg AF: Paroxetine. In: Comprehensive textbook of psychiatry, 6th edition. Kaplan HI, Sadock BJ. Williams and Wilkins, Baltimore, 1994.

Dunner DL: An overview of paroxetine in the elderly. Gerontology 1994;1:21-27.

Gram LF: Fluoxetine. N Engl J Med 1994;331:1354-1361.

Greenberg RP, Bornstein RF, Zborowski MJ et al: A meta-analysis of fluoxetine outcome in the treatment of depression. J Nerv Ment Dis 1994;182:547-551.

Grimsley SR, Jann MW: Paroxetine, sertraline, and fluvoxamine: New selective serotonin reuptake inhibitors. Clin Pharm 1992;11:930-957.

Klieser E, Lehmann E, Heinrich K: Fluoxetine in patients with major depressive disorder: A responder analysis. Pharmacopsychiatry 1995; 28:14-19.

Schatzberg AF: Dosing strategies for antidepressant agents. J Clin Psychiatry, May 1991;52:(suppl)5,14-20.

Schatzberg AF, Cole JO: Manual of clinical psychopharmacology. American Psychiatric Press, 2nd edition, Washington, DC, 1991.

Stokes PE: Fluoxetine: A five-year review. Clinical Therapeutics, March/April, 1993;15(2):216-243.

Wilde MI, Plosker GL, Benfield P: Fluvoxamine: An updated review of its pharmacology and therapeutic use in depressive illness. Drugs 1993; 46(5):895-924.

NOTES

#6 Selective Serotonin/Norepinephrine Re-uptake Inhibitors

The trend toward developing more selective drugs that have equal efficacy to older agents but fewer side effects has spawned the selective serotonin norepinephrine re-uptake inhibitors (SNRIs). Venlafaxine (Effexor) is the first of these drugs that is available on the American market. Similar drugs, including duloxetine, are in various stages of development at this time, and there are likely to be more available in the coming years.

Venlafaxine (Effexor), released in 1994, has received considerable attention in the lay press. Because of its dual action on norepinephrine as well as its serotonin re-uptake, it has been referred to as Prozac with a punch or "Prozac plus" in some lay articles. Indeed, venlafaxine may have some potentially significant advantages over other newer antidepressants, including SSRIs, atypicals, and $5HT_2$ antagonists, in the treatment of major depression (see Table 6.1). Although it may be a less favorable choice for some patients, venlafaxine appears to be an important addition to the growing arsenal of antidepressants.

6.

Mechanism of Action

Venlafaxine strongly inhibits the re-uptake of serotonin and norepinephrine. To some extent, this mechanism of action parallels that found in tricyclic antidepressants, such as imipramine (Tofranil). However, there appear to be several important differences that distinguish venlafaxine from tricyclics and other antidepressants.

The most important difference may be the selectivity of venlafaxine. Tricyclic antidepressants

TABLE 6.1 — **Profile of Venlafaxine (Effexor)**

Potential Advantages of Venlafaxine (Effexor)	1. May be more effective than the SSRIs in some serious forms of depression. 2. Fewer potential drug interactions in venlafaxine relative to other antidepressants secondary to low inhibition of hepatic enzymes and weak protein binding.
Potential Disadvantages of Venlafaxine (Effexor)	1. Divided dosing may be less convenient for some patients. 2. Blood pressure should be monitored with venlafaxine treatment.

interfere with other neurotransmitters, such as acetylcholine and histaminic receptors. Like SSRIs, venlafaxine has little affinity for these receptors and, thus, tends to be better tolerated than cyclic drugs and is similar in side effect profile to SSRIs.

Another distinguishing feature of venlafaxine is its apparent immediate effect on down-regulating beta adrenergic receptors. This down-regulation (see Section #4) is often associated with clinical response and usually requires days to weeks of repeated antidepressant administration before significant changes in the receptors are evident.

Venlafaxine is the only antidepressant tested thus far that seems to cause significant down-regulation of beta receptors after the first dose. At this time there are not enough data to determine whether this rapid down-regulation of beta receptors will translate into more rapid onset of clinical response with venlafaxine.

Indications

Venlafaxine has been well studied for the treatment of major depression. Several outpatient studies have demonstrated that it is superior to placebo and is at least as effective as the antidepressants to which it has been compared. Venlafaxine also has been found to be effective for patients with more serious depressive episodes, including inpatients with melancholic features. Although it is a new drug, venlafaxine probably has been better studied for the treatment of more severe depression than have SSRIs.

Because venlafaxine has a dual action on monoamine neurotransmitters, there is some speculation that it may be useful for depressed patients who have not responded to other treatment regimens. There are preliminary data that support the use of venlafaxine in refractory major depression; however, it is too early to determine how useful venlafaxine will be in this population.

Venlafaxine should be useful for other psychiatric conditions treated by SSRIs, including:

- Obsessive compulsive disorder
- Panic disorder
- Eating disorders
- Attention deficit disorder
- Borderline personality disorder
- Certain pain conditions

There are open label studies of the utility of venlafaxine in all these disorders. Unfortunately, no double-blind, controlled studies have yet been performed to determine the utility of venlafaxine in conditions other than major depression.

Side Effects and Their Management

The side effect profile of venlafaxine (see Table 6.2) is generally superior to that of older antidepressants and is comparable to SSRIs. The drug does not appear to cause anticholinergic effects such as the dry mouth and constipation that plague users of tricyclic drugs. Its lack of antihistaminic effects also indicates that weight gain and sedation are not major problems. Like SSRIs, venlafaxine does not seem to produce the orthostatic drop in blood pressure that can be problematic with tricyclic antidepressant and MAOI use.

Nonetheless, venlafaxine has its fair share of side effects. Nausea may be somewhat more prevalent with venlafaxine than with most SSRI use. Approximately 33 percent of patients experience nausea early in treatment; nausea is the most common reason patients give for discontinuing treatment. Patients typically adapt to this side effect in the first four weeks of treatment, however; so it is important for patients to be reassured that these symptoms will likely subside completely in time. As with SSRIs, taking the medication with food often helps reduce nausea and GI upset.

Insomnia and somnolence are the next most common reasons patients give for discontinuing venlafaxine treatment. About 20 percent of patients complain of insomnia versus only 10 percent of patients treated with placebo. Likewise, somnolence occurs in approximately 25 percent of patients on venlafaxine. Both side effects tend to be dose-related, and some adaptation may occur over the first few weeks of treatment. As with SSRIs, shifting the dose to earlier in the day may alleviate insomnia and shifting it to later in the day may deter somnolence.

Venlafaxine shares several side effects with SSRIs, such as:

- Excessive perspiration
- Headaches
- Agitation
- Sexual dysfunction

Treatment-emergent increases in blood pressure is the only side effect seen in venlafaxine that is relatively uncommon with SSRI use. This effect is dose-related and is probably mediated by the noradrenergic effects of the drug. Approximately 13 percent of venlafaxine patients on doses of 300 mg per day or more showed treatment-emergent increases in blood pressure, while only three percent of those taking 100 mg per day or less experienced this effect. The increases in blood pressure occurring in patients taking the maxi-

TABLE 6.2 — **Common Side Effects of Venlafaxine (Effexor)**

Gastrointestinal	Nausea
CNS Depression	Somnolence
CNS Activation	Agitation Insomnia
Sexual Dysfunction	Decreased libido Delayed orgasm
Hypertension	Modest increases in blood pressure
Other	Excessive perspiration Headaches

mum dose (375 mg per day) are fairly modest, with an average increase in diastolic pressure of 7.2 mm Hg at six weeks and with no significant changes seen for the same duration at doses of 75 and 225 mg per day. Less than one percent of patients in premarketing studies discontinued the drug because of sustained increases in blood pressure, and the blood pressure returned to baseline levels with discontinuation of the drug. Still, it is prudent for clinicians to check patients' blood pressure at every visit, particularly in the first two months of venlafaxine treatment. Because changes in blood pressure are dose-dependent, a reasonable strategy is first to lower the dose if a significant increase in blood pressure is noted. Anecdotally, some clinicians have successfully employed small doses of beta-blockers or calcium channel blockers in patients who do less well on lower doses of venlafaxine but have sustained increases in blood pressure. Further study is needed to determine the optimal strategy for dealing with treatment-emergent increases in blood pressure in the relatively few patients for whom this is a more serious problem.

Drug Interactions

The potential for drug interactions with venlafaxine use is less than that with SSRI and most antidepressant use. This weaker interaction potential appears to be due to a lessened effect on the cytochrome P_{450} system and weak protein binding.

The most serious potential interaction with venlafaxine, as with SSRIs, is its use with MAOIs. Venlafaxine should not be used concurrently with MAOIs because of the risk of serotonin syndrome developing. Discontinuing venlafaxine for two weeks prior to starting treatment with an MAOI should be safe.

Venlafaxine appears to be metabolized, at least in part, by the cytochrome P_{450} IID_6 isoenzyme. Drugs that inhibit IID_6, such as SSRIs, may raise serum levels of venlafaxine but lower the levels of venlafaxine's active metabolite, keeping the total plasma concentration of venlafaxine fairly constant. Thus, recent studies indicate that venlafaxine can be safely administered with IID_6 inhibitors.

Unlike SSRIs, venlafaxine appears to be a weak inhibitor of the IID_6 isoenzyme. In fact, venlafaxine appears to be 10 to 300 times less potent an inhibitor of this hepatic enzyme than SSRIs. Thus, venlafaxine appears to have much less potential for raising serum levels of drugs such as risperidone, tricyclics, and class IC antiarrhythmics than have SSRIs (see Section #5).

In addition, venlafaxine does not appear to be an inhibitor of other hepatic enzymes, such as $IIIA_{3/4}$. Nefazodone (Serzone) and fluvoxamine (Luvox) are fairly potent inhibitors of $IIIA_{3/4}$ and can significantly raise serum levels of drugs such as terfenadine (Seldane) and astemizone (Hismanil). This is not a small matter, since more potent inhibitors of $IIIA_{3/4}$, such as ketokonazole, have been associated with fatalities when combined with terfenadine by raising serum levels of the allergy medicine and inducing fatal arrhythmias. Venlafaxine does not appear to carry a significant risk of interacting with drugs dependent on $IIIA_{3/4}$.

Caffeine, which is fairly ubiquitous in coffee, soft drinks, and chocolate, is metabolized via the IA_2 enzyme. Venlafaxine is not an inhibitor of this enzyme, unlike fluvoxamine (Luvox) and some other SSRIs. Thus, venlafaxine should not prove too stimulating for patients who have higher caffeine intakes.

Benzodiazepines are partially dependent on the IIC_{19} isoenzyme for their metabolism. Venlafaxine does not appear to inhibit the metabolism of drugs such as diazepam. SSRIs may be weak inhibitors of IIC_{19}.

Venlafaxine differs from other antidepressants in that it is not tightly bound to serum proteins. Most antidepressants, including tricyclics and SSRIs, are more than 85-percent bound to protein. Venlafaxine is only about 30-percent bound. This would suggest that venlafaxine is less likely to displace other drugs that are tightly bound, such as warfarin and oral contraceptives.

Dosing

Venlafaxine has a relatively short half-life (about four hours for the drug and 11 for its active metabolite) and thus should be taken in divided doses. Twice-a-day dosing seems to be adequate, but some patients will better tolerate three doses per day at the highest doses.

Unlike SSRIs, for which the dose response curve is flat, venlafaxine demonstrates a positive dose-response relationship, i.e., higher doses are clearly associated with a higher percentage of responders. However, higher doses may also be associated with more side effects.

Most patients respond to doses in the 75 to 225 mg per day range. This should be the target range for the vast majority of outpatients. However, more seriously depressed patients often benefit from the highest dose range of 300 to 375 mg per day.

The usual starting dose is 37.5 mg twice a day. Patients with severe liver or kidney disease require lower doses because they will clear venlafaxine less efficiently. The manufacturer suggests that the dose need not be lowered in elderly patients; however, many psychiatrists start these patients at 25 mg per day and increase the dose gradually, since older patients tend to be more sensitive to toxic effects of all drugs, including venlafaxine.

A typical regimen for titrating the dosage increase is to initiate treatment at 75 mg per day for two to three weeks. If there is limited response, the dose may be increased by 75 mg per week until a dose of 225 mg per day is achieved. More depressed patients often require the higher doses of 300 to 375 mg per day.

Discontinuing Venlafaxine

Discontinuing venlafaxine seems to result in withdrawal symptoms similar to those associated with SSRIs, including:

- Nausea
- Fatigue
- Headaches
- Dizziness

Because the half-life of venlafaxine is relatively short, a slow taper may be more important for this drug than for longer-acting drugs such as fluoxetine. Withdrawal symptoms may occur after only one week of treatment but appear to be uncommon and mild.

While there are no specific guidelines for tapering the drug, the manufacturer advises tapering the dose over a two-week period when the medication is administered for six weeks or longer.

References:

Cantu TG, Korek JS, Romanoski AJ: Focus on venlafaxine: A new option for the treatment of depression. Hosp Formul 1994;29(1):25-33.

Clerc GE, Ruimy P, Verdeau-Palles J: A double-blind comparison of venlafaxine and fluoxetine in patients hospitalized for major depression and melancholia. The Venlafaxine French Inpatient Study Group. Int Clin Psychopharmacol 1994;9:139-143.

DeBattista C: Venlafaxine in the treatment of depression: Practical considerations. Psych Times Jan 1995;12:(1).

Ellingrod VL, Perry PJ: Venlafaxine: A heterocyclic antidepressant. Am J Hosp Pharm 1994;51:3033-3046.

Esherefsky L: Drug interactions involving antidepressants: Focus on venlafaxine. J Clin Psychopharmacol 1996;16(3, suppl 2):37s-53s.

Guelfi JD, White C, Magni G: A randomized, double-blind comparison of venlafaxine and placebo in patients with major depression and melancholia. Clin Neuro 1992;15(suppl 1, Pt B):323B.

Holliday SM, Benfield P: Venlafaxine: A review of its pharmacology and therapeutic potential in depression. Drugs 1995;49:280-294.

Khan A, Fabre LF, Rudolph R: Venlafaxine in depressed outpatients. Psycho Bull 1991; 27(2):141-144.

Moyer J, Andree T, Haskins JT, Husbands G, Muth E: The preclinical pharmacological profile of venlafaxine: A novel antidepressant agent. Clin Neurop 1992;15(suppl 1, Pt.B):435B.

Nierenberg AA, Feighner JP, Rudolph R et al: Venlafaxine for treatment-resistant unipolar depression. J Clin Psychopharmacol 1994;14:419-423.

Rudolph R, Entsuah R, Derivan A: Early clinical response in depression to venlafaxine hydrochloride. Biol Psyc 1991;29(suppl 11S):324B.

Rudorfer MV, Manji HK, Potter WZ: Comparative tolerability profiles of the newer versus older antidepressants. Drug Saf 1994;10:18-46.

Schweitzer E, Feighner J, Mandos LA, Rickels K: Comparison of venlafaxine and imipramine in the acute treatment of major depression in outpatients. J Clin Psy 1994;55(3):104-108.

Schweizer E, Weise C, Clary C, Fox I, Rickels K: Placebo-controlled trial of venlafaxine for the treatment of major depression. J Clin Psycho 1991; 11(4):233-236.

Troy S, Piergies A et al: Venlafaxine pharmacokinetics and pharmacodynamics. Clin Neurop 1992;15(suppl 1, Pt. B):324B.

#7 5-HT_2 Antagonists

Trazodone (Desyrel), released to the American market in 1981, represented the first serotonin specific antidepressant. It is not, however, a classic selective serotonin re-uptake inhibitor (SSRI). While it does block the re-uptake of serotonin to some extent, this does not appear to be the drug's primary action. In addition, its side effect profile differs significantly from that of SSRIs.

Recently, trazodone was joined by a related compound, nefazodone (Serzone), which offers a better side effect profile than trazodone in many respects and appears to be an effective antidepressant.

Nefazodone and trazodone have a pharmacological profile that allows for good antianxiety effects, favorable effects on sleep, and low incidence of sexual dysfunction.

TABLE 7.1 — **The 5-HT_2 Antagonist Antidepressants**

Drug	Starting Dose	Therapeutic Dose
Trazodone (Desyrel)	50-150 mg/day	200-600 mg/day
Nefazodone (Serzone)	100-200 mg/day	300-600 mg/day

However, these drugs are generally taken in divided doses and, as with any antidepressant, will not be tolerated by all patients

Mechanism of Action

Of the subtypes of serotonin receptors recently characterized, trazodone and nefazodone appear to block, or antagonize, the 5-HT_2 receptor and to have both anxiolytic antidepressants properties. They appear to have other actions on serotonin, including blocking its reuptake, but thise appears less significant than the direct action as serotonin receptor antagonists.

Nefazodone differs from trazodone in several important respects. It lacks the antihistamine effect that makes trazodone more sedating, and it is not an α-2 antagonist that may contribute to priapism in some trazodone patients. Nefazodone also lacks the strong α-1 properties that result in hypotension with trazodone use. Neither drug has significant anticholinergic effects.

Indications

The primary indication for trazodone is treatment of major depression. Despite many studies demonstrating trazodone's antidepressant effects, some clinicians suggest the drug is less robust in those effects than other medications. In many cases, the lack of efficacy attributed to trazodone may be the result of inadequate dosing.

Trazodone's sedating effect may be useful for treating major depressive episodes that have prominent insomnia or anxiety features. Some anecdotal reports suggest that trazodone may also be useful for panic disorder, and there are controlled data that indicate it is as effective as librium in treating generalized anxiety disorder. Some clinicians have found that small amounts of trazodone (50 mg two or three times daily with food) may be substituted for benzodiazepine in treating generalized anxiety.

Trazodone is commonly used as a general sleeping agent and in doses as low as 25 to 100 mg per day appears to be an effective hypnotic. Patients using the drug as a sleep agent tend not to feel groggy when they awaken in the morning, though larger doses can cause excessive daytime sedation. An advantage of trazodone over benzodiazepine is that it does not appear to be addictive.

Trazodone has been used in combination with SSRIs to offset the activating properties of agents such as fluoxetine and may ease agitation and insomnia associated with fluoxetine use. In addition, because it acts directly on serotonin receptors, trazodone may augment the antidepressant effects of SSRIs; this use needs further study.

Like trazodone, the primary indication for nefazodone (Serzone) is treatment of major depression. Nefazodone has been studied and found to be effective for both outpatients with mild to moderate depression and inpatients with more serious depression. There is some preliminary data that the drug may alleviate some sleep problems without causing excessive sedation. In addition, nefazodone has shown significant utility in attenuating anxiety symptoms often associated with depression. Preliminary data also suggest its use for premenstrual dysphoria.

Potential Drug Interactions

Trazodone and nefazodone are serotonergic agents that may cause serotonergic syndrome when used concurrently with MAOIs. MAOIs should be stopped two weeks prior to starting treatment with 5-HT_2 antagonists.

Trazodone is a potent blocker of α-adrenergic receptors and thus may produce orthostatic drops in blood pressure when patients rise suddenly from sitting or supine positions. This appears less problematic with nefazodone use. Caution should be exercised when trazodone is used concurrently with antihypertensives. The combination may cause dramatic orthostatic hypotension, increasing the risk of falls, particularly in the elderly.

Because trazodone is sedating, it can potentiate the effects of other sedating agents, such as benzodiazepines and alcohol.

Neither nefazodone nor trazodone is a potent inhibitor of the IID_6 hepatic enzymes described in Section #6. Nefazodone tends to be a potent inhibitor of the $CYIIIA_{3/4}$ liver enzyme, which is responsible for metabolizing some benzodiazepines, such as alprazolam (Xanax) and triazolam (Halcion), and also breaks down commonly prescribed antihistamines, such as terfenadine (Seldane) and astemizole (Hismanil). Concurrent use of nefazodone with any of these drugs will likely increase blood levels of the antihistamines and benzodiazepines. Concurrent use of nefazodone and alprazolam or triazolam requires lowering the dose of benzodiazepine.

The combination of astemizole or terfenadine with nefazodone is contraindicated, because preventing metabolism of these drugs may result in lethal arrhythmias, such as Torsades de Pointes. Nefazodone is probably similar to fluvoxamine in its ability to inhibit the $CYIIIA_{3/4}$ isoenzyme. Ketoconazole is more potent at inhibiting this enzyme than any antidepressant and has been associated with a number of fatalities when used in combination with terfenadine. Although nefazodone should be less problematic than ketokonazole, concurrent use of terfenadine, astemizone, and cisapride is contraindicated due to a potential for arrhythmias.

Side Effects and Their Management

The 5-HT_2 antagonists appear to be well tolerated and apparently are safe in overdose when not used with other drugs. Nefazodone and trazodone are not particularly anticholinergic or antihistaminic and appear to be safe for patients with cardiac disease, though trazodone has been associated rarely with arrhythmias in patients with pre-existing premature ventricular contractions.

These drugs do not typically produce the sexual dysfunction or insomnia associated with SSRIs.

Because of its sedating properties, trazodone is probably best taken at night, 30 minutes to one hour before bedtime. Taking the drug with food may slow absorption and attenuate sedation to some extent. It should not be taken before driving or operating heavy machinery. At higher doses, patients occasionally experience some motor incoordination.

In contrast, nefazodone at low doses is less sedating than trazodone; however, at doses in the 300 to 600 mg range, about 28 percent of patients complain of somnolence, twice the rate experienced by plalcebo-treated patients. Thus, patients taking high doses should be advised to be careful when performing tasks that require attention, such as driving.

The most common serious side effect of trazodone is orthostatic hypotension, which appears to be dose-related and more problematic with geriatric patients. Orthostasis may be the cause of the dizziness and lightheadedness associated with trazodone use, but the risk of syncope and dizziness appears to increase if the drug is not taken with food.

Adequate hydration and support stockings may help mitigate this effect. Clinicians should check supine and standing blood pressures while the dosage is being adjusted upwards, and patients should be advised to rise slowly from sitting and supine positions. Nefazodone appears less likely than trazodone to produce orthostatic hypotension (about 25 percent of patients) but may be associated with a dose-related increase of dizziness and lightheadedness.

While trazodone is rarely associated with the delayed orgasm and ejaculation common with SSRI use, it is associated with the rare occurrence of priapism, a sustained, painful erection that, in approximately 33 percent of cases, requires surgical intervention to prevent permanent impotence (intracavernosal injection of epinephrine sometimes alleviates priapism). This side effect may result from α-adrenergic blockade, which affects less than one in 50,000 trazodone male patients. Patients, particularly young males, should be advised to report frequent or prolonged erections in the absence of sexual stimuli; a painful erection of greater than 30 minutes' duration should be evaluated in an emergency room. In such cases, the trazodone should be discontinued.

Gastrointestinal side effects, such as nausea and diarrhea, are less common with 5-HT_2 antagonist than with SSRI use. However, in early treatment or with high doses, patients are occasionally bothered by gastric irritation and nausea when the drug is taken on an empty stomach. Taking medications with food often helps mitigate gastric upset; eventual habituation to this effect will occur.

Nefazodone occasionally is associated with afterimages and other visual distortions. These effects may be attributed to the drug's active metabolite, M-CPP, which is responsible for the dysphoric activation sometimes seen in early treat-

TABLE 7.2 — **Side Effects of $5HT_2$ Antagonists**

Cardiovascular	Orthostatic hypotension (much greater in trazodone than nefazodone)
CNS Depression	Sedation Somnolence (greater in trazodone than nefazodone)
Gastrointestinal	Constipation Nausea Upset stomach
Neurological	Dizziness Headaches Lightheadedness
Other Autonomic	Blurred or abnormal vision Dry mouth

ment. M-CPP levels are higher in those who metabolize the IID_6 isoenzyme slowly or who have recently used SSRIs. The best strategy appears to be to lower the dose and increase it gradually.

Dosing

For antidepressant use, trazodone is typically initiated at 50 to 150 mg per day. Patients, particularly older ones, who do not tolerate 150 mg per day may be initiated at half a 50-mg tablet per day. Although the manufacturer recommends divided doses, many clinicians give all or most of the medication at night to diminish daytime sedation and somnolence. The dose may be increased by 50 mg every three days until a dose of 200 to 300 mg per day is achieved.

There is little evidence that doses greater than 400 mg per day are of more benefit than lower doses. In fact, patients on these high doses frequently do less well than patients in 150 to 300 mg per day range. The decrease in efficacy at higher doses may be secondary to the side effects outweighing the drug's therapeutic benefit or to a possible therapeutic window for the drug. Though the manufacturer suggests benefits of doses as high as 600 mg per day, high doses are rarely used in clinical practice.

Because nefazodone is less sedating and is less likely to cause orthostatic hypotention than trazodone, patients tend to tolerate it at a higher starting dose. The usual starting dose is 100 mg twice daily; however, many clinicians find the drug to be better tolerated at starting doses of 50 mg twice daily. The dose may be increased by 100 mg per week until doses in the 300 to 600 mg per day range are achieved. In premarketing studies, the mean dose for outpatients with major depression was approximately 400 mg per day in divided doses. Geriatric patients and those sensitive to side effects may be started at 50 mg at night for three days and the doses increased by 50 mg every three to five days.

Discontinuing the 5-HT_2 Antagonists

Withdrawal symptoms appear to be uncommon when discontinuing trazodone, though, as with most antidepressants, some case reports describe withdrawal syndrome associated with rapid discontinuance. Nefazodone, trazodone, and their active metabolites are relatively short-acting and are cleared fairly rapidly when their use is discontinused. These effects may contribute to such withdrawal symptoms as:

- Headaches
- Insomnia
- Nausea
- Anxiety
- Malaise

These symptoms may stem from a serotonergic or adrenergic rebound when trazodone is stopped abruptly. While no reports of withdrawal symptoms associated with nefazodone exist to date, the occasional patient may experience some symptoms from sudden withdrawal of the drug. No guidelines exist for tapering either nefazodone or trazodone, but it appears prudent to taper the dose no more quickly than it was titrated up; decreasing the dose of either drug by no more than 100 mg per week seems reasonable.

References:

Armitage R, Rush AJ, Trivedi M et al: The effects of nefazodone on sleep architecture in depression. Neuropsychopharmacology 1994;10:123-127.

Eison AS, Eison MS, Torrente MS et al.: Nefazodone: Preclinical pharmacology of a new antidepressant. Psychopharm Bull 1990;26(3): 311-315.

Fabre LF, Feighner JP: Long-term therapy for depression with trazodone. J Clin Psychiatry 1983;44:17.

Fontaine R: Novel serotonergic mechanisms and clinical experience with nefazodone. Clin Neuropharm 1993;16(suppl 3):S45-50.

Nierenberg A: Possible trazodone potentiation of fluoxetine: A case series. J Clin Psychiatry 1992;53:83-85.

Otani A et al.: Mechanism of the development of trazodone withdrawal symptoms. Int Clin Psychopharmacology 1994(Summer);9(2):131-133.

Rickels K, Schweizer E, Clary C et al.: Nefazodone and imipramine in major depression: A placebo controlled trial. Br J Psychiatry 1994;164:802-805.

Scharf MB, ed.: Insights in the use of trazodone in depressed patients. J Clin Psychiatry 1990;51(9 suppl):2.

Thompson JW, Ware MR, Blashfield RK: Psychotropic medication and priapism: A comprehensive review. J Clin Psychiatry 1990;51:430.

#8 Atypical Antidepressants

The antidepressant medications described thus far share properties with at least one other agent that is on the market or is expected to be marketed. Antidepressants are usually classified by chemical structure or mechanism of action, but there always appear to be some antidepressant agents that do not fit neatly into any class of drugs.

Currently, bupropion (Wellbutrin) is such an antidepressant agent. It is chemically unrelated to the cyclic drugs, SSRIs, MAOIs, or the 5-HT_2 antagonists and does not appear to share its mechanism of action with other classes of antidepressant agents. Therefore, it is often referred to as an atypical antidepressant.

Initially, it was suggested that bupropion worked by increasing the availability of dopamine in the brain. Drugs that do this have long been associated with mood-elevating properties. (Some street drugs, such as methamphetamine and cocaine, may be mood-elevating secondary to their ability to enhance dopamine.) However, few prescription antidepressants have been strong dopamine re-uptake inhibitors; and the one exception, nomifensine, was removed from the market in 1986 secondary to its association with hemolytic anemia. Bupropion, released again in 1988, is a much weaker dopamine re-uptake blocker; in fact, it is not at all clear that bupropion's effect on dopamine has anything to do with its antidepressant effects. Regardless, bupropion is an effective antidepressant with a fairly favorable side effect profile.

Another drug which is expected to be released in the near future that also has a unique mechanism of action is mirtazapine (Remeron). The mechanism of action of this tetracyclic drug distinguishes it from other tricyclic or tetracyclic compounds. Mirtazapine appears to be a selective noradrenergic antagonist that offers a useful alternative to currently available antidepressants.

Indications

Unlike most antidepressants, bupropion has been used almost exclusively for treatment of major depression and has been shown to be useful in treating the atypical subtype (see Section #15) in at least two studies. In addition, it has been suggested that bupropion is less likely than other antidepressants to induce mania in susceptible patients. This remains to be seen; studies both support and refute this suggestion. There are similar suggestions that bupropion may be less useful in psychotic depression because of its tendency to potentiate dopamine at high doses. In practice, this does not occur, because bupropion tends only to potentiate dopamine at doses considerably higher than the maximum dose of 450 mg per day.

Panic disorder does not appear to be particularly responsive to bupropion treatment. Bupropion may be quite activating, and patients with anxiety disorders are frequently sensitive to activating drugs. Therefore, bupropion may not be the best choice for patients with prominent anxiety features or insomnia. However, some reports show that patients with treatment-resistant panic have done well on bupropion. Bupropion has also proven useful in several studies of Attention Deficit Disorder (ADD) in children.

Mirtazapine has been studied in Europe as a treatment for major depression, including more seriously depressed inpatients and those in anxiety states. An FDA advisory panel recently recommended that mirtazapine be approved for the treatment of major depression.

Mechanism of Action

It remains unclear how bupropion acts as an antidepressant. It has no significant serotonin or norepinephrine re-uptake properties, has no effects on monoamine oxidase, and is not a 5-HT antagonist.

Its dopamine re-uptake properties tend to be most evident at doses above 600 mg per day, which is considerably higher than the maximum recommended dose of 450 mg per day. In addition, the dopamine re-uptake properties of bupropion are more closely associated with exacerbating psychoses than with antidepressant effects. Recent research demonstrated that the main neurotransmitter effect of bupropion may be on the noradrenergic system.

Bupropion has some amphetamine-like metabolites; a single dose of 400 mg is associated with a mild amphetamine-like response. However, bupropion is usually taken in divided doses that do no exceed 150 mg, so an addictive "buzz" should not occur.

Mirtazapine differs from available antidepressants in that it is a selective α-2 autoreceptor antagonist. Since activation of α-2 receptors inhibits the release of norepinephrine, mirtazapine blocks the receptor and therefore enhances norepinephrine release. The drug also has some effects on other noradrenergic receptors including α-1, but these appear to be less prominent than mirtazapine's effect on α-2.

Side Effects and Their Management

Bupropion appears to be well tolerated and has a side effect profile that offers advantages over other first-line agents. Sexual dysfunction appears to be uncommon in bupropion treatment. Thus, bupropion may be a good treatment alternative for patients with pre-existing sexual dysfunction and for those who cannot tolerate the sexual side effects of SSRIs and venlafaxine.

Likewise, gastrointestinal side effects, such as nausea and diarrhea, rarely occur with bupropion treatment. Weight gain is uncommon, though 28 percent of bupropion patients report a weight loss of five pounds or more, particularly in the first two months of treatment. The mild anorectic effects of the drug may make it more attractive to patients concerned with weight gain and less attractive to patients with significant anorexia secondary to depression. Most patients, however, regain the weight.

Bupropion has no significant cardiotoxic effects and is not anticholinergic. As with other first-line agents, bupropion appears to be relatively safe in overdose compared to cyclic drugs and MAOIs.

The most common side effects of bupropion are those related to CNS activation, including agitation and anxiety. While up to 33 percent of patients complain of feeling more agitated while taking the drug, less than two percent are so distressed by the symptom that they discontinue treatment. Because taking the day's final dose before bedtime may interfere with the ability to fall asleep, the medication may be taken earlier in the evening. As with other activating antidepressants, small doses of benzodiazepines, such as lorazepam (Ativan) 0.5 mg twice a day, can significantly ease the side effects of bupropion in the first few weeks of treatment; thereafter, most patients adapt to the CNS stimulating effects of the drug.

Mirtazapine appears to be a generally well tolerated antidepressant without many of the side effects that occur with serotonergic antidepressants. For example, there appears to be much less gastrointestinal distress with mirtazapine than with SSRIs. However, mirtazapine is associated with the orthostasis, dizziness, and vertigo that might be expected from its alpha-blocking properties. In addition, mirtazapine has more anticholinergic-like side effects than SSRIs, including constipation and dry mouth. It might be anticipated that sexual dysfunction may be less of a problem with mirtazapine than with SSRIs but there are no data on this issue. The most common side effect of mirtazapine is somnolence, with 54 percent of patients experiencing some sedation. Increased appetite and weight gain were the next most common side effects.

TABLE 8.1 – **Common Side Effects of Bupropion (Wellbutrin)**

• CNS activation
  • Agitation
  • Anxiety
  • Irritability
• Tremor
• Mild anorexia and weight loss

Another mildly annoying side effect bupropion shares with some antidepressants is tremor, which occurs in about 20 percent of patients. Tremor is dose-related and rarely results in patients' discontinuing treatment. Still, some patients are bothered by tremor, which may be reduced by lowering the dose or adding propranolol (Inderal) at 10 to 20 mg two or three times a day.

The most serious potential side effect of bupropion is seizure, which occurs in about four of every 1,000 cases at doses below the maximum recommended dose of 450 mg per day. The incidence of seizure at therapeutic doses is somewhat higher with bupropion than other antidepressant use. When the dose is increased to the 450 to 600 mg per day range, the incidence of seizure increases about tenfold, to four in 100 cases. Therefore, bupropion should not be used in doses above 450 mg and should be avoided in patients with histories of seizure disorder.

Similarly, doses greater than 150 mg taken at one time may enhance the risk of seizure. Bupropion should be used with caution in patients predisposed to seizure, including patients with a history of:

- Head trauma
- Stroke
- Eating disorders, such as bulimia

Potential Drug Interactions

The potential for serious drug interactions appears to be limited with bupropion (see Appendix). There is a theoretical concern that bupropion taken concurrently with MAOIs may produce a hypertensive crisis, since dopaminergic agents have been frequently associated with this serious side effect. Therefore, the manufacturer recommends discontinuing MAOI treatment at least two weeks prior to starting bupropion treatment. However, there are no case reports of MAOI/bupropion interactions in the literature.

Bupropion is extensively metabolized in the liver and is capable of inducing its own metabolism. Thus, other hepatic drug inducers, such as cimetidine (Tagamet) and carbamazepine (Tegretol), theoretically could decrease serum levels of bupropion, requiring an increase in the bupropion dose.

Since bupropion has no significant CNS depression effects of its own, it appears to be safe in combination with other CNS depressants such as alcohol. There is one report that bupropion can counteract sedation and decrease concentration of ethanol but not the subjective sense of inebriation. Nonetheless, since the seizure threshold is lowered by withdrawal from all CNS depressants, special vigilance is required in patients who discontinue alcohol or benzodiazepine use while concurrently taking bupropion.

Mirtazapine is sedating and, in combination with alcohol and other CNS depressants, may be cumulative. Because the drug is metabolized via IIDC and $3A_{3/4}$, drugs that compete for these 150 enzymes, including the SSRIs and nefazodone, would be expected to increase mirtazapine levels.

Dosing

The usual starting dose of bupropion is 100 mg twice a day. If no significant side effects are noted, the dose may be increased to 100 mg three times a day after three or four days. A dose of 150 mg twice a day is a reasonable alternative that will probably enhance compliance without substantially increasing the risk of seizure. Patients should not take more than 150 mg of bupropion at a time secondary to seizure risk. Most patients respond to 300 mg per day, though some appear to respond to higher doses. If no response is seen after three weeks of bupropion, the dose may be increased by 100 mg per week to a maximum dose of 450 mg per day in three divided doses.

Mirtazapine is started 15 mg per day at bedtime. If no response is seen at two weeks, the dosage should be increased by 15 to 30 mg per day. The maximum dose is 45 mg per day. The drug has a half-life of 20 to 40 hours; thus once a day dosing is sufficient. In the largest study done to date, the mean dose in patients with moderate to severe depression was about 50 mg per day.

Discontinuing Atypical Agents

There are no reports in the literature of withdrawal symptoms associated with discontinuing bupropion. Some patients at the Mood Disorders Clinic at Stanford University have reported a significant increase in dysphoria with the sudden discontinuance of bupropion (Wellbutrin). However, it is difficult to say whether this represents a withdrawal effect or a relapse of pre-existing dysphoria. Nevertheless, it may be prudent for patients to taper the discontinuance of bupropion at a rate of no more than 100 mg per week.

At this time there are no data on the discontinuation of mirtazapine. However, adrenergic rebound has been reported with rapid discontinuance of other noradrenergic antidepressants, and it is prudent to taper the drug until more is learned about the optimal way to stop it.

References:

Calabrese JR, Markovitz PJ: Treatment of depression: New pharmacological approaches. Prim Care 1991;18:421-426.

Davidson J: Seizures and bupropion: A review. J Clin Psychiatry 1989;50:256.

Feighner JP, Gardner EA, Johnston JA et al.: Double-blind comparison of bupropion and fluoxetine in depressed outpatients. J Clin Psychiatry 1991;52:329.

Hamilton MJ et al.: The effects of bupropion, a new antidepressant, on alcohol and their interaction in man. Eur J Clin Pharm 1984;27:75

James WA: Bupropion: Overview and prescribing guidelines in depression. South Med J 1991; 84:222.

Smith WT, Glaudin V, Panagides J et al: Mirtazapine vs amitriptyline vs placebo in the treatment of major depressive disorder. Psychopharmacol Bull 1990;26:191-196.

Vartiainen H, Leinonen E: Double-blind study of mirtazapine and placebo in hospitalized patients with major depression. Eur Neuropsychopharmacol 1994;4:145-150.

van Moffaert M, de Wilde J, Vereecken A et al: Mirtazapine is more effective than trazodone: A double-blind controlled study in hospitalized patients with major depression. Int Clin Psychopharmacol 1995;10:3-9.

NOTES

1.	Diagnosis of Major Depression	Diagnosis
2.	Differential Diagnosis of Depression	
3.	Laboratory Studies in Depression	
4.	Antidepressant Medications	Treatment
5.	Selective Serotonin Re-uptake Inhibitors	
6.	Selective Serotonin/Norepinephrine Re-uptake Inhibitors	
7.	$5\text{-}HT_2$ Antagonists	
8.	Atypical Antidepressants	

#9 Cyclic (Tricyclic and Tetracyclic) Antidepressants

The tricyclic and tetracyclic antidepressants, named because of their cyclic chemical structure, are the among the oldest and best studied class of antidepressants. While many antidepressants have at least one ring in their chemical structure, the cyclic antidepressants referred to in this text have a three- or four- ringed structure. This class includes:

- Tertiary amine tricyclic antidepressants (TCAs):
  - Amitriptyline (Elavil)
  - Imipramine (Tofranil)
- Secondary amine tricyclics (derivatives of tertiary amine
  - Nortriptyline (Pamelor)
  - Desipramine (Norpramin)
- Tetracyclic (four-ringed) medications:
  - Amoxapine (Asendin)
  - Maprotiline (Ludiomil)

In many respects, the tricyclic antidepressant agents are the gold standard by which the efficacy of newer antidepressants is measured. These antidepressants have been so thoroughly investigated for the treatment of depression that no new antidepressant is approved before at least one study suggests that the novel agent compares favorably in efficacy to them.

While there is no substantial evidence that the multicyclic antidepressants are more efficacious than newer agents, the multicyclic agents clearly have been better studied in more serious forms of depression. Few studies have been conducted,

FIGURE 9.1 – **Structural Formula of Imipramine and Amoxapine**

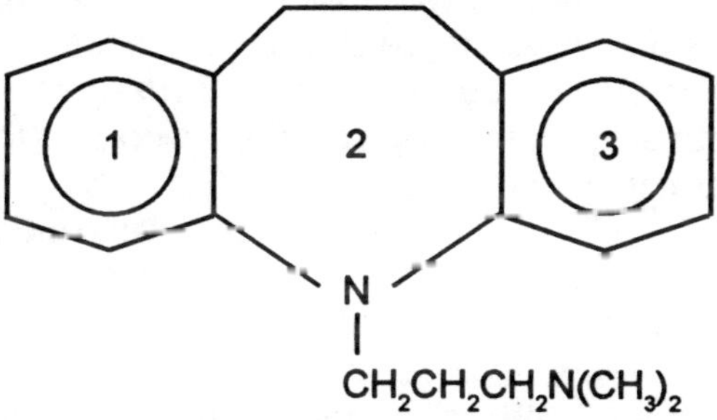

Imipramine (Tricyclic)

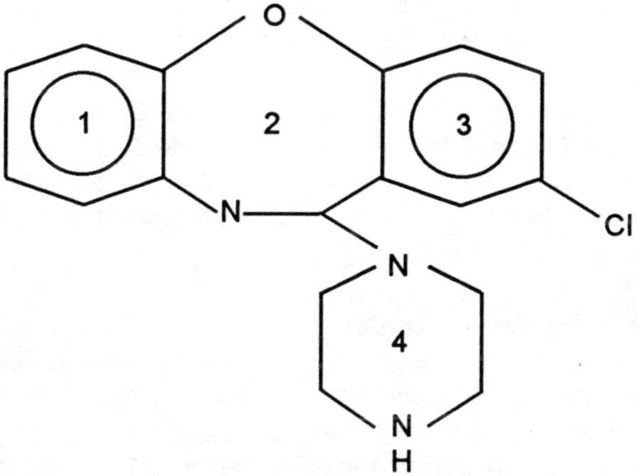

Amoxapine (Tetracyclic)

9.

for example, on the efficacy of SSRIs in the treatment of psychotic or melancholic depression, but virtually all studies in the past 30 years have supported the role of tricyclic antidepressants for these more serious depressive episodes. Thus, some psychiatrists argue that it may be more prudent initially to use tricyclic antidepressants in the treatment of some forms of depression than to try relatively untested drugs.

It is not efficacy, however, but safety and side effect profiles that have relegated the cyclics to second-line status in the treatment of most depression. All cyclic drugs are potentially lethal in overdose, and the dose required for fatality is relatively low; approximately 1500 mg of imipramine (Tofranil), a one-week supply at therapeutic doses, can prove lethal in most patients.

There is little doubt that the newer antidepressants tend to be better tolerated than the cyclic drugs. Typically, far fewer patients have dropped out of studies secondary to side effects when treated with SSRIs, serotonin antagonists, or venlafaxine (Effexor) than when treated with cyclic antidepressants. Nonetheless, many patients who do well with cyclic drugs cannot tolerate the side effects of the newer drugs.

Mechanism of Action

The cyclic antidepressants most closely resemble venlafaxine in mechanism of action. They all block re-uptake of serotonin and norepinephrine to some extent, the effect believed to account for the efficacy of cyclic agents in treating depression.

The problem is that cyclic antidepressants are fairly non-selective in their actions. Not only do they block the re-uptake of neurotransmitters that appear to be important to treatment but they also block a number of other neurotransmitters, producing bothersome side effects. The drugs also tend to be potent antihistamines, to block acetylcholine, and to produce orthostatic hypotension by blocking adrenergic sites.

Indications

The cyclic antidepressants are FDA-approved primarily for the treatment of major depression, and they have been successfully used to treat all forms of major depression and dysthymia. In addition, clomipramine (Anafranil) is currently FDA-approved for treating obsessive compulsive disorder (OCD). The serotonin system is thought to play an important role in the etiology of this disorder, and patients with obsessive thoughts and compulsions to repeat behaviors, such as hand washing, have historically been difficult to treat. Clomipramine is the most potent serotonin re-uptake inhibitor among cyclic drugs. Fluoxetine (Prozac) and fluvoxamine (Luvox) have also received FDA approval for treatment of OCD. All SSRIs are useful in treating this disabling disorder.

For more than 30 years the TCAs have been first-line agents for the treatment of panic disorder, and there is evidence that cyclic drugs are also effective in treating generalized anxiety disorder and agoraphobia.

Insomnia frequently responds to low doses of amitriptyline (Elavil) and other sedating cyclic antidepressants.

Since cyclic antidepressants are not addictive, they may be safer to use than tranquilizers in patients with significant abuse potential. Of course,

TABLE 9.1 — **Cyclic (Tricyclic and Tetracyclic) Antidepressants**

Drug	Starting Dose	Therapeutic Dose	Manufacturer
Amitriptyline (Elavil)	25 mg	150 – 300 mg	Stuart
Amoxapine (Asendin)	50 mg	200 – 400 mg	Lederle
Clomipramine (Anafranil)	25 mg	100 – 250 mg	Basel
Desipramine (Norpramin)	25 mg	150 – 300 mg	Marion Merrell Dow

continued ⇩

Doxepin (Sinequan)	25 mg	150 – 300 mg	Roerig
Imipramine (Tofranil)	25 mg	150 – 300 mg	Geigy
Nortriptyline (Pamelor)	10 – 25 mg	50 – 150 mg	Sandoz
Protriptyline (Vivactil)	10 mg	15 – 50 mg	Merck and Co.
Trimipramine (Surmontil)	25 mg	150 – 300 mg	Wyeth-Ayerst

use of cyclic drugs for treating anxiety states and insomnia has to be balanced against their less favorable side effect and safety profiles.

The cyclic antidepressants also have made their way into the arsenals of many non-psychiatric physicians. Imipramine (Tofranil), amitriptyline (Elavil), and doxepin (Sinequan) are commonly used to treat a variety of pain conditions, including diabetic neuropathy and fibromyalgia.

In addition, TCAs are commonly used in low doses for the prophylaxis of migraine headaches. The tricyclics, particularly doxepin, are quite antihistaminic and have been used in treating peptic ulcer disease and gastroesophageal reflux.

Additionally, the TCAs have quinidine-like properties at therapeutic doses and have been used, in rare instances, to treat arrhythmias.

Drug Interactions

Since cyclic drugs are relatively "dirty" (i.e., have many actions other than those necessary for efficacy), there is generally more potential for drug interactions with their use than with newer, more selective drugs. The combination of more serotonergic antidepressants, such as clomipramine (Anafranil), may result in a fatal serotonergic syndrome. Since all cyclics have some serotonergic properties, it is probably prudent that patients be advised to avoid use of any cyclic antidepressant concurrently with MAOIs. Still, the combination of TCAs and MAOIs is sometimes successfully used to treat depressed patients for whom other treatments have failed.

SSRIs can inhibit the metabolism of TCAs, thereby increasing serum levels and toxicity of these drugs; SSRIs may increase serum levels of TCAs by a factor of eight or more. Serious toxicity, including arrhythmia, has occasionally been reported when a cyclic drug is combined with an SSRI. Desipramine (Norpramin) and other TCAs are sometimes combined with fluoxetine (Luvox) in patients who have not responded to one agent alone. This combination may be successful, but it requires close monitoring of TCA serum levels and an occasional ECG to monitor cardiac conduction.

The interaction of cyclic drugs and cardiac depressants, such as digitalis and quinidine, may be problematic, since TCAs have their own quinidine-like properties. The combination of a TCA with some cardiac-depressant drugs may compound cardiac depression and irritability. Occasional cardiac arrests and fatalities have resulted from these interactions.

Since all cyclic drugs are potentially sedating, they can enhance effects of other sedating agents, including benzodiazepines, barbiturates, and alcohol. Likewise, cyclic antidepressants can potentiate the respiratory depression associated with narcotics. Also, the anticholinergic effects of cyclic drugs tend to be additive in combination with other anticholinergic agents such as diphenhydramine (Benadryl) and certain antipsychotic drugs like chlorpromazine (Thorazine).

Cyclic drugs can antagonize and reduce the efficacy of some antihypertensive medications. For example, much of the efficacy of guanethidine (Ismelin) may be lost when a TCA is added. Decreased antihypertensive efficacy has also been noted when a TCA is combined with clonidine (Catapres). Diuretics, beta-blockers, calcium channel blockers, and other antihypertensives appear to be reasonable alternatives to use with cyclic agents. However, all antihypertensives may en-

TABLE 9.2 — **Common Side Effects of Cyclic Antidepressants**

Cyclic Antidepressant	Common Side Effect
Anticholinergic	Dry mouth, urinary retention, constipation, esophageal reflux, blurred vision
Adrenergic Blockade	Orthostatic hypotension
Antihistamine Effects	Weight gain, sedation
CNS Activation	Agitation, insomnia, restlessness (more common in secondary amines; protriptyline, desipramine, nortriptyline)
Cardiac	Nonspecific EKG changes, prolonged conduction time, tachycardia

hance the orthostatic hypotension associated with cyclic antidepressants and, therefore, need to be used with caution in the elderly.

Side Effects and Their Management

The side effects of cyclic antidepressants frequently limit their utility. Most side effects occur in the first five weeks of therapy, and many depressed patients are never able tolerate therapeutic doses of these drugs because the side effects force them to discontinue treatment prematurely. Geriatric patients have a particularly difficult time with the side effects of this class of drugs.

One advantage that cyclic drugs may have over all other antidepressants is the availability of serum levels that may predict efficacy and toxicity. Obtaining blood serum levels of most antidepressants appears to be worthless. For example, there is so much individual variability in serum levels of patients taking SSRIs that they are of no predictive value in assessing the risks of side effects or predicting a therapeutic dosage. Several cyclic agents, however, appear to have therapeutic windows (see Table 9.3), plasma levels below which the chance of efficacy is reduced and above which the chance of toxicity is enhanced. With this class of drugs, nortriptyline (Pamelor) has the clearest therapeutic window.

Anticholinergic side effects, particularly dry mouth and constipation, are among the most common reasons patients give for discontinuing treatment with cyclic antidepressants (see Table 9.2).

Sometimes these side effects can be reversed by incorporating a procholinergic drug, bethanechol, into the regimen at 25 to 50 mg three times a day. Pilocarpine drops in a four-percent solution administered twice a day may alleviate blurred vision; a more diluted pilocarpine solution, one-percent or more, may be used as a mouthwash several times a day for dry mouth. Some patients change their eyeglass prescriptions for improved vision once a therapeutic dose of the antidepressant is established.

The elderly are particularly susceptible to anticholinergic effects of these drugs. Amitriptyline (Elavil) and protriptyline (Vivactil) are the most anticholinergic cyclic antidepressant; nortriptyline (Pamelor) and desipramine (Norpramin) are among the least. Thus, nortriptyline and desipramine are among the best tolerated antidepressants in their class and should be considered for most patients before other cyclic compounds are initiated.

Orthostatic hypotension is a potentially serious side effect of cyclic antidepressants. The orthostasis, a result of α–adrenergic blockade, may result in patients falling and seriously injuring themselves. Elderly patients have sometimes broken hips and died secondary to falls resulting from orthostasis. Prudence dictates that clinicians check both sitting and standing blood pressures in elderly patients on cyclic antidepressants. It is also important that geriatric patients be warned about the possibility of orthostatic hypotension and advised to rise from sitting or supine positions slowly. Support stockings often help elderly patients contend with postural changes in blood pressure.

The antihistamine effects of cyclic drugs are more annoying than they are dangerous. These effects include sedation and weight gain. Sedation is best combated by taking medications at bedtime, though some patients feel groggy upon awakening in the morning; for these patients, the dose may have to be decreased. Weight gain is a difficult problem in some patients. Careful attention to diet and exercise will help. Amitriptyline (Elavil) and doxepin (Sinequan) are among the most antihistaminic TCAs; nortriptyline (Pamelor) and desipramine (Norpramin) are among the least.

Cardiac toxicity is the most serious complication of cyclic antidepressants, which have a quinidine-like effect and can impair cardiac conduction. Malignant arrhythmias are the leading cause of death in acute overdose, so caution must be exercised when these drugs are prescribed for patients with pre-existing conduction defects such as left-bundle branch blocks; such patients may be at particular risk for malignant ventricular arrhythmias. Since pre-existing conduction defects may not be apparent, a baseline EKG should be obtained before cyclic antidepressant treatment is initiated and repeated after therapeutic dosage is achieved.

Some of the newer cyclic compounds have their own unique side effects in addition to those they share with their drug class. For example, maprotiline (Ludiomil) and clomipramine (Anafranil) may be associated with an increased risk of seizure at higher doses. Amoxapine (Asendin), a chemical cousin of the antipsychotic medication loxapine can produce side effects secondary to dopamine blockade, including galactorrhea and such extrapyramidal symptoms as drug-induced Parkinson's disease and some involuntary movements (tardive dyskinesia).

Dosing Strategies

Given the potential for toxicity with cyclic antidepressants, it is generally best to adopt the "start low and go slow" dictum toward dosing. A conservative approach is to initiate treatment of imipramine (Tofranil) at 50 mg a day at bedtime and to maintain this dose for one week. The dose can then be increased by 25 mg every two or three days. After one to two weeks at 150 mg per day, the dose may be increased by 50 mg per week until a maximum dose of 300 mg per day is achieved. A similar approach may be used in dosing amitriptyline (Elavil), desipramine (Norpramin), doxepin (Sinequan), and trimipramine (Surmontil).

Nortriptyline (Pamelor) can generally be initiated at 50 mg per day and increased by 50 mg a week, as tolerated, to a maximum dose of 150 mg per day. Plasma levels can be obtained once the patient is at a 75 mg per day dose to help gauge the need for further increases. Most patients will be in the therapeutic range between 50 and 100 mg per day.

Amoxapine (Asendin) has a higher maximum dose than the other cyclic antidepressants and seems frequently to require titration to higher doses to achieve a satisfactory response. Its typical starting dose is 150 mg per day, and it can be increased by 75 mg per week, as tolerated, until the maximum dose of 400 mg per day is achieved.

If inadequate response is seen after six to eight weeks of treatment with therapeutic doses of a cyclic agent, another agent may need to be added to the regimen (see Section #16) or a switch of drug class may be required. Generally, there is little value in switching patients to another cyclic compound if one cyclic antidepressant is not successful.

TABLE 9.3 — **Therapeutic Plasma Level Ranges for Tricyclic Drugs**

Drug	Blood Level (ng/ml)
Amitriptyline (Elavil)	100 – 250
Desipramine (Norpramin)	150 – 300
Doxepin (Sinequan)	120 – 250
Imipramine (Tofranil)	150 – 300
Nortriptyline (Pamelor)	50 – 150
Protriptyline (Vivactil)	75 – 250

As with all antidepressants, elderly patients and patients with extensive liver or renal disease should be treated with lower doses. A reasonable rule of thumb is to initiate compromised patients at half the usual starting dose and raise the level slowly to half the usual maximum dose.

Discontinuing Cyclic Antidepressants

The cyclic antidepressants may be associated with withdrawal symptoms when treatment is stopped suddenly. Typical symptoms include:

- Fatigue
- Malaise
- Nausea
- Flu-like symptoms

These symptoms, which may begin a day or two after the medication is stopped and continue for a week, have often been attributed to the "cholinergic rebound" that occurs after the long-standing blockade of acetylcholine is suddenly removed. Predictably, the more anticholinergic agents, such as amitriptyline (Elavil), are frequently implicated with withdrawal symptoms.

While most patients do not experience significant withdrawal symptoms, tapering the more anticholinergic cyclic drugs slowly is recommended. Recent practice suggests erring on the side of maintaining patients on their antidepressants rather than allowing them to discontinue use rapidly. Most patients easily tolerate decreasing doses by 25 percent per week so that the medication is completely discontinued in one month's time.

References:

Amsterdam J, Brunswick D, Mendels J: The clinical application of tricyclic antidepressant pharmacokinetics and plasma levels. Am J Psychiatry 1980;137:653-662.

Asberg M, Cronholm B, Sjoqvist F et al.: Relationship between plasma level and therapeutic effect of nortriptyline. Br Med J 1971;3:331-334.

Bielski RJ, Friedel RO: Prediction of tricyclic antidepressant response. Arch Gen Psychiatry 1976;33:1479-1489.

Biggs JT, Spiker DC, Petit JM et al.: Tricyclic antidepressant overdose: Incidence and symptoms. JAMA 1977;238:135-138.

Boston Collaborative Drug Surveillance Program: Adverse reactions to the tricyclic antidepressants. Lancet 1972;1:529-531.

Everett HC: The use of bethanechol chloride with tricyclic antidepressants. Am J Psychiatry 1975;132:1202-1204.

Gram LF, Christiansen J, Overo KF: Pharmacokinetic interaction between tricyclic antidepressants and other psychopharmaca. Acta Psychiatr Scand 1973;(suppl)243:52-53.

Klerman GF, Cole JO: Clinical pharmacology of imipramine and related antidepressant compounds. Pharmacol Rev 1965;17:101-141.

Roose SP, Glassman AH: Cardiovascular effects of tricyclic antidepressants in depressed patients. J Clin Psychiatry, Monograph Series 1989;7(2):1-18.

Shopsin B; Second generation antidepressants. J Clin Psychiatry 1980;41(12):45-46.

NOTES

#10 Monoamine Oxidase Inhibitors

In the 1950s, the first reports on the antidepressant properties of a drug called iproniazid were published. This drug, chemically related to the tuberculosis drug isoniazid, was the first monoamine oxidase inhibitor (MAOI) to be used in the treatment of depression, and it essentially opened the door for modern antidepressant drug development.

Currently, three MAOIs are still available on the American market:

- Phenelzine (Nardil)
- Tranylcypromine (Parnate)
- Selegiline (Eldepryl), the anti-Parkinson's disease drug, more recently released

With the advent of more benign antidepressant drugs, MAOIs are now relegated to third-line status for treating depression, after the newer antidepressants and cyclic drugs. MAOIs remain an important treatment option for some depressive episodes but are hampered by the need for dietary restrictions, the potential for lethal drug interactions, and frequent side effects with their use. Fortunately, studies are underway on new, more selective, and reversible MAOIs that may mitigate some problems associated with the currently available drugs.

Indications

MAOIs are FDA-approved primarily for depression that has not responded to other treatment. Their use has been studied for mild and serious forms of depression, and there is literature

TABLE 10.1 — **The Monoamine Oxidase Inhibitors (MAOIs)**

Drug	Starting Dose	Therapeutic Dose	Manufacturer
Phenelzine (Nardil)	15 – 30 mg	45 – 90 mg	Parke-Davis
Selegiline (Eldepryl)	5 – 10 mg	20 – 60 mg	Somerset/Sandoz
Tranylcypromine (Parnate)	10 mg	20 – 40 mg	SmithKline

supporting its use for melancholic depression and depression unresponsive to other treatment. In addition, there is much literature suggesting that these drugs are more useful than cyclic drugs in treating the atypical subtype of depression characterized by mood reactivity, hypersomnia, and overeating (see Section #15). Some psychiatrists believe MAOIs are among the most effective antidepressants for depression characterized by significant anxiety or panic attacks.

MAOIs are used for several other psychiatric disorders. For example, they continue to be used for treatment of panic disorder, agoraphobia, and sometimes bulimia; and MAOIs are said frequently to be more effective than cyclic antidepressants in the treatment of dysthymia.

The primary indication for MAOIs outside psychiatry is for treatment of Parkinson's disease. Selegiline (Eldepryl) is used for this disorder due to its tendency to enhance central dopamine at low doses. At these low doses (5 to 10 mg per day), selegiline is fairly selective for MAO-A, which also acts on norepinephrine and serotonin and has a lower risk for serious interactions. Higher doses (20 to 60 mg per day), however, are needed to treat depression, but the drug loses its selectivity at these doses. Thus, antidepressant doses of selegiline are associated with all the other problems common to MAOIs.

Mechanism of Action

MAOIs limit the ability of an enzyme, monoamine oxidase, to break down dopamine, serotonin, and norepinephrine. Thus, they increase the availability of monoamine neurotransmitters in the synaptic cleft. Unfortunately, they also irreversibly inhibit MAO throughout the body; once the enzyme is inhibited by an MAO drug, enzymatic activity is lost for the two weeks or longer required to produce more monoamine oxidase. This is why MAOIs must be discontinued two weeks prior to lifting dietary restrictions or initiating serotonergic antidepressants.

A reversible MAOI would circumvent this problem. There are at least two types of monoamine oxidase. Monoamine oxidase A, found primarily in nerve terminals and the gut, acts primarily on norepinephrine and serotonin. Monoamine oxidase B, found in blood platelets, acts preferentially on phenylethylamines. It should be possible to develop truly selective monoamine oxidase A inhibitors that do not require dietary restrictions. Unfortunately, all currently available MAOIs are non-selective at therapeutic antidepressant doses.

Side Effects and Their Management

Orthostatic hypotension is one of the most common side effects of MAOIs. This side effect probably results from the influence of the drug on the availability of norepinephrine in the sympathetic system. Patients taking MAOIs should be checked at office visits for both sitting and standing blood pressures and should be advised to rise from sitting and supine positions slowly and to drink plenty of fluids to help prevent falls. Support stockings sometimes help mitigate postural hypotension.

Although the MAOIs are not particularly anticholinergic, dry mouth and constipation may occur in 20 percent of patients taking these drugs. Often conservative management, including bulk laxatives for constipation and chewing gum for dry mouth, will suffice to counteract these side effects.

TABLE 10.2—**Common Side Effects of the MAOIs**

- Cardiovascular:
  - Orthostatic hypotension
- CNS activation:
  - Insomnia, restlessness (particularly with tranylcypromine [Parnate] use)
- CNS depression:
  - Sedation, somnolence (particularly with phenelzine [Nardil] use)
- Anticholinergic symptoms
  - Dry mouth, constipation
- Sexual dysfunction:
  - Impotence, delayed orgasm
- Other:
  - Weight gain, muscle cramps

Some patients find MAOIs to be activating and may complain of agitation and insomnia. Shifting the dose to earlier in the day is sometimes effective in alleviating these effects. Phenelzine (Nardil) is more sedating and less activating than tranylcypromine (Parnate) and, therefore, may be a better choice for patients sensitive to activating agents. Some psychiatrists add lorazepam (Ativan) at 0.5 mg two or three times a day to the regimen to help combat agitation and insomnia; low doses of other benzodiazepines should be well tolerated and equally effective. Reducing the dosage of MAOIs often is necessary to ease the activating properties.

A rare but serious side effect of MAOIs may occur if patients consume foods high in tyramine. Since MAO is responsible for the breakdown of tyramine in the gut, these patients may absorb

TABLE 10.3 — **Foods High in Tyramine that Should be Avoided by Patients on MAOIs**

Category	Foods
Fermented Meats/Fish	Caviar, pickled herring, sardines Sausages, aged salami, summer sausage Liver – chicken and beef
Aged Cheeses	Blue, Brie, Camembert, Cheddar, Liederkranz, Swiss (Cottage and cream cheese are acceptable)
Aged Wines	Chianti and red wines
Others	Caffeine in high doses, i.e., espressos, large quantities of colas or chocolates, over-the-counter caffeine preparations such as Vivarin, No-Doze Brewer's yeast Fruits – figs and ripe avocados

large amounts into their bloodstreams, where it can act as a false neurotransmitter and produce a dangerous increase in blood pressure. This "hypertensive crisis" may result in lethal complications such as stroke or myocardial infarction. Patients taking MAOIs should be given a list of foods to avoid; those unable to comply with the dietary restrictions are not safe candidates for MAOI treatment (see Table 10.3).

A hypertensive crisis can present with the symptoms of malignant hypertension, including violent headaches, confusion, and delirium. Some psychiatrists provide their patients with a supply of nifedipine and instruct them to take 10 to 20 mg sublingually if a serious headache develops. A more prudent strategy may be to educate patients on the clinical manifestations of a surge in blood pressure and instruct them to get to the nearest emergency room if these symptoms develop.

Potential Drug Interactions

Patients treated with MAOIs should not take other medications, including over-the-counter drugs, without first consulting their treating physicians. The list of medications that interact with MAOIs is lengthy.

Three classes of medications are particularly problematic when combined with MAOIs and should be avoided, the most important being the serotonergic agents (see Sections #5 and #6). The selective serotonin re-uptake inhibitors and clomipramine (Anafranil), when combined with MAOIs, also may produce a serotonergic syndrome that occasionally progresses to delirium, coma, hyperpyrexia and even death.

Another class of agents that reacts dangerously to MAOIs is the sympathomimetic drugs. Elicit drugs, such as cocaine, methamphetamine, and dexedrine, frequently produce hypertensive crises when combined with MAO drugs. Unfortunately, many over-the-counter cold preparations, including ephedrine, pseudoephedrine, oxymetazoline (Afrin), and phenylephrine, may cause the same problem. Although cold preparations tend to be less problematic than elicit drugs, they are more commonly used. Many cold preparations have warning labels instructing patients to consult their physicians if they arc taking antidepressants. This warning applies almost exclusively to MAOIs.

Analgesics are sometimes associated with hyperpyrexia, seizures, and serotonergic symptoms when combined with MAOIs. By far, the most serious interactions have involved meperidine (Demerol), to which several fatalities have been attributed when taken in combination with MAOIs. On the other hand, most narcotics, including morphine and codeine, have been used concurrently with MAOIs without problems.

Certain antihypertensives, including guanethidine (Ismelin), methyldopa (Aldomet), and reserpine, have produced paradoxical hypertension when combined with MAOIs. All antihypertensives may worsen the orthostatic hypotension secondary to MAOIs, but diuretics and calcium channel blockers appear to be safer alternatives for the treatment of high blood pressure.

Dosing Strategies

Given the side effects, particularly hypotension, of MAOIs, the dose of these drugs must be titrated carefully. Blood pressures, including orthostatic pressures, should be monitored as the medication is adjusted.

Phenelzine (Nardil) may be initiated at 15 mg twice a day and may be increased to 15 mg three times a day after three days at the lower dose. Subsequently, the dose may be increased by 15 mg per week until the maximum dose of 90 mg per day in divided doses is achieved. Most patients require doses in the 60 to 90 mg per day range. A greater portion of the daily dose taken at night will mitigate some sedation and orthostasis effects.

For tranylcypromine (Parnate), the starting dose is typically 10 mg in the morning and 10 mg in the early afternoon. Bedtime doses should generally be avoided to limit the risk of worsening insomnia. The dose can be increased by 10 mg per week in divided doses until a maximum of 40 mg per day is achieved. Many patients do well with 10 to 30 mg per day, though some patients benefit from higher doses.

Selegiline (Eldepryl) appears to be a somewhat weaker antidepressant than other MAOIs, though it may be valuable in treating depression in patients with Parkinson's disease. The incidence of depression in this patient population is high, and selegiline is a logical choice for an antidepressant trial. Selegiline is typically initiated at 5 to 10 mg per day and increased to 20 mg per day in the second week of treatment. Thereafter, the dose may be increased by 10 mg per week until a maximum dose of 50 mg per day is achieved.

Discontinuing Monoamine Oxidase Inhibitors

Withdrawal symptoms appear to be uncommon with MAOIs. It is generally more prudent to taper than abruptly discontinue any antidepressant. The main point in discontinuing MAOIs is that dietary restrictions and cautions about drug interactions must continue after the drug is stopped. Approximately two weeks is required for the enzyme monoamine oxidase to regenerate after an MAOI is discontinued. During this two week period, catastrophic drug interactions and hypertensive crises can still occur.

References:

Kline NS: Clinical experience with iproniazid. J Clin and Experimental Psychopathology 1958; 19:72-78.

McCabe B, Tsuang MT: Dietary considerations in MAO inhibitor regimens. J Clin Psychiatry 1982;43:187-81.

McGrath PJ, Stewart JW, Harrison W et al.: Treatment of melancholia with tranylcypromine. Am J Psychiatry 1984;141:288-289.

Pearlstein T, Frances AJ, Kocsis JH et al.: A controlled study of the antidepressant efficacy and side effects of Deprenyl: A selective monoamine oxidase inhibitor. Arch Gen Psychiatry 1989;46:45-50.

Quitkin F, Rabkin A, Klein DF: Monoamine oxidase inhibitors. Arch Gen Psychiatry 1979;36:749-760.

Robinson DS, Nies A, Ravaris CL et al.: Clinical pharmacology of phenelzine. Arch Gen Psychiatry 1978;35:629-635.

Switching MAOIs. Biological therapies in psychiatry 1984;7(9):33-36.

Teicher MH, Cohen BM, Baldessarini RJ et al.: Severe daytime somnolence in patients treated with an MAOI. Am J Psychiatry 1988;145:1552-1556.

NOTES

#11 Electroconvulsive Therapy

History

Electroconvulsive therapy (ECT), one of the oldest continuing treatments in psychiatry, involves a series of applications of a small amount of electric current through the scalp to induce generalized seizures. ECT is generally regarded as one of the single most effective treatments for severe major depression and some other serious psychiatric disorders. Convulsive therapy was originally described by the Hungarian physician Meduna in 1934 as an effective treatment for what is now known as schizophrenia. In 1938, an Italian team, Bini and Cerletti, described the use of electrical currents instead of chemicals, such as camphor oils, to produce reliable seizures in psychiatric patients and reported impressive remissions of psychotic symptoms. The news of a potentially effective treatment for psychosis, at a time when no such treatments were available, swept the Western world; and by the early 1940s ECT was being practiced at many centers throughout North America.

There were many problems with ECT's introduction to North America. It was introduced at a time when controlled studies were not the standard by which efficacies of new treatments were assessed. Virtually all the reports on ECT efficacy in the 1940s and '50s were anecdotal case reports.

A related problem was that ECT was used indiscriminately in its early years. Since careful studies were not performed and clinical guidelines did not exist, physicians were free to use ECT for any conditions they believed could be relieved by the procedure. A review of the literature of that period reveals that ECT was endorsed for everything from alcoholism to character pathology. In addition, uncontrollable patients, regardless of their diagnoses, were sometimes considered candidates for ECT. While punitive use of ECT was not as common as popular media depictions would suggest, ECT was undoubtedly misused at times.

The early use of ECT was rather crude. Originally, the procedure was performed without benefit of anesthesia. It usually involved the use of hand-held leads, and patients were often not sedated at all. Attendants stood by the bedside to limit patients' risk of injury secondary to flailing about in the clonic phase of the generalized seizure. Among the most common injuries were compression fractures of the vertebral bodies, broken teeth, and injured limbs.

With these various problems and the introduction of effective antipsychotic drugs and antidepressants in the 1950s and '60s, ECT use began to wane substantially and, in fact, almost became extinct. However, in the late 1970s and '80s, ECT began to experience a resurgence. One reason for its renewal was the clear evidence of its effectiveness for patients who did not respond to available medications. A second major factor was data that demonstrated ECT's safely in treating depression and other disorders.

Good controlled studies were completed during this time, and the data suggested that ECT was generally more effective than pharmacotherapy in the treatment of depression. Refinements in the procedure, particularly the advent of anesthesia in conjunction with ECT, made the procedure less frightening and reduced its risk for serious complications. ECT is currently integrally employed in most academic psychiatric services and many community hospitals.

The ECT Procedure

While ECT sounds frightening, the procedure is much less dramatic than many procedures in modern medicine. Typically, patients are first evaluated by laboratory studies, including a 12-lead EKG and chemistry panel. Generally, assigned anesthesiologists review these studies, perform pre-operation physicals, and discuss patients' laboratory studies and procedure risks with treating psychiatrists. Second opinions are often obtained regarding the need for ECT.

Once the decision is made to pursue the procedure, patients are scheduled for a series of treatments. In the United States, treatments are most commonly scheduled every other day; a Monday, Wednesday, Friday schedule is typical, but the optimal interval between treatments remains unknown.

ECT is performed in a variety of settings, including operating recovery rooms, alternative therapy units, and specialized ECT suites. Patients are attached to monitors for continuous readings of cardiac, respiratory, and blood pressure status; intravenous lines and the EEG and electrode leads are placed. The electrode leads may be hand-held or attached with a band, and lead placement may be unilateral in the non-dominant hemisphere or bilateral (see Figure 11.1). Patients then are given a barbiturate sleeping agent.

Blood pressure cuffs are often used as tourniquets on the arm or leg to prevent the paralytic

FIGURE 11.1 – Bilateral Placement of Electrode Leads in ECT

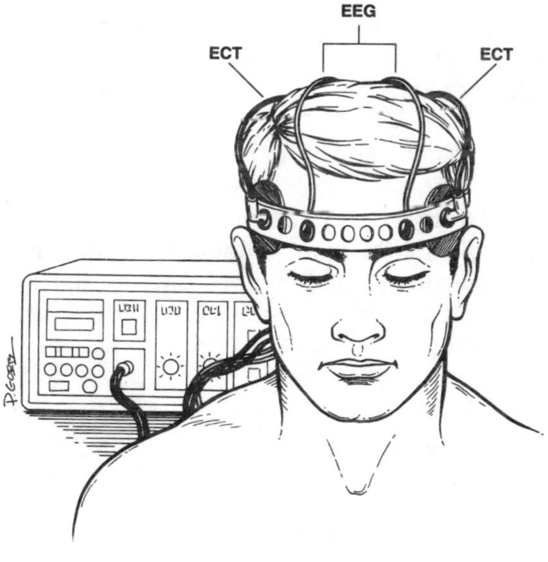

agent, usually succinylcholine, from flowing down the arm. This allows the seizure to be monitored physically, since patients' muscles are paralyzed and motor activity is typically seen only in the cuffed limb. Once patients are asleep and their muscles are completely relaxed, a pulse of the electrical stimulus is administered. The amount of electricity required is small, usually enough to light a 20-watt light bulb for a few seconds. An adequate seizure continues for 30 to 90 seconds and is manifested by mild tonic-clonic activity in the cuffed limb and by spike and wave activity on the EEG. With the seizure over, patients typically awaken within minutes. Patients continue to be monitored for 45 to 90 minutes at which time most patients are alert, oriented, and ready to return to their wards or go home.

Indications

Several consensus reports, including the American Psychiatric Association Task Force Report on ECT in 1990, have concluded that ECT is a safe and effective treatment for several disorders. By far, its most common use in the U.S. is for treating major depression. Most studies have found ECT to be superior to antidepressant therapy, at least in the short-run. According to a review by the Royal College of Psychiatrists in 1977, the marked response rate to ECT for major depression was 70 to 76 percent in several multicenter studies as opposed to a response rate of less than 50 percent for treatment with tricyclic antidepressant and MAOIs. For psychotic or delusional depression, the difference in response rate may be greater. In some studies, the response rate of psychotic depression to ECT was twice that to conventional antidepressant drug therapy. Thus, in many centers, ECT is the treatment of choice for psychotic depression.

A less common indication for ECT is for treatment of mania. Several effective treatments for mania exist, including lithium and antipsychotic drugs, and ECT is currently rarely used to abort a manic episode. However, though no controlled studies on ECT use for mania exist, several retrospective studies suggest that manic patients have had quick and favorable responses to ECT. ECT has been employed a number of times for manic patients in the first trimester of pregnancy, during which mood-stabilizing drugs, particularly lithium, are associated with teratogenic effects on the unborn child. Many clinicians have concluded that it is safer for these patients and their unborn children to complete a series of ECT treatments than for the mother to take potentially toxic drugs. Evidence to date suggests that ECT may be safely performed in the first trimester of pregnancy.

A third potential indication for ECT is for treatment of some forms of schizophrenia. Schizophrenia that is antipsychotic-resistant and is characterized by persistent affective symptoms, such as depression, sometimes responds well to ECT. Likewise, catatonia, in which patients assume rigid postures, often responds well to ECT. In general, however, the response rate to ECT is lower and more transient for schizophrenia than for depression.

Less well studied ECT applications include its use in the treatments of:

- Some movement disorders, such as Parkinson's disease

- Refractory seizures (short-term treatment)
- Neuroleptic malignant syndrome associated with antipsychotic use

While major depression is the main indication for ECT use, the criteria for employing it in major depression remain ambiguous (see Table 11.1). ECT is typically not considered a first-line treatment; however, severe depressions, such as psychotic depression, are increasingly popular exceptions to this rule. Similarly, severe depressive episodes in geriatric patients are increasingly being treated with ECT as first-line therapy.

Mechanism of Action

Despite more than 60 years of study, no one really knows how ECT works. Studies have demonstrated that repeated seizures produce many of the effects on monoamine neurotransmitters and their receptors that are seen with chronic antidepressant drug therapy, and it is assumed that this is the basis for the efficacy of ECT. However, generalized seizures produce a myriad of complex chemical/hormonal effects, and it has not been possible to isolate the crucial variables definitively.

In any case, seizure duration appears to be an important factor in ECT efficacy. Seizure duration of less than 15 seconds may be associated with cognitive side effects but also with less therapeutic benefit. Most clinicians regard an adequate individual seizure as being 30 to 90 seconds in duration.

Single seizures appear to be generally inadequate in producing a therapeutic response for depression. Rather, a series of treatments, usu-

TABLE 11.1 — **Suggested Criteria for ECT Use in Major Depression**

1. Antidepressant medications have not been tolerated or pose a significant medical risk.
2. Antidepressant medication trials have not been successful.
3. ECT has been successful in previous episodes.
4. Catatonia is present.
5. A rapid response is needed because of imminent suicide risk or patient's health has been significantly compromised by the depressive episode (i.e., severe cachexia secondary to depression, inability to attend to the activities of daily living).
6. Psychotic features, such as delusions and hallucinations, are present concurrently.

ally with at least one day between sessions, is necessary. In major depression, six to 12 ECT treatments of at least 30 seconds' duration per treatment is necessary for maximum benefit.

Side Effects and Their Management

ECT appears to be a remarkably safe procedure. It has a mortality rate of approximately four in 10,000 cases, a rate similar to that seen with barbiturate anesthesia alone. When the rare fatality occurs, its usual cause is a cardiovascular event, such as malignant arrhythmia or myocardial infarction.

While the risk of a serious adverse effect is low, there are several common side effects of ECT. It is not unusual, for example, for patients to experience headache for several hours after the procedure; the headache is usually mild, often responds to non-steroidal agents such as acetaminophen or aspirin, and is gone by the evening or following day.

Typical anesthetic agents employed in ECT include a barbiturate sedative, such a methohexital or thiopental, and a paralytic agent, such as succinylcholine. Patients may have side effects from these agents, including muscle soreness from the succinylcholine. Non-steroidal analgesic agents usually help, as does switching to another paralytic agent.

The most common side effects of ECT are short-term cognitive deficits. Some deficits are sequelae of all seizures, idiopathic or induced. The period immediately after a generalized seizure (the postictal state) is marked by some confusion and memory loss. The confusion usually lasts for an hour or so after the treatment but may be more dramatic in patients who are elderly, who are taking certain medications such as lithium, and whose seizures continue for longer than 90 seconds. Rarely patients may be delirious for a day or two after treatment.

Memory loss is one of the more frightening potential side effects of ECT. Difficulties remembering things that happened just prior to ECT treatment (retrograde memory loss) and difficulties learning new material immediately after treatment (anterograde memory loss) is universal sequelae of generalized seizures. The memory loss is usually confined to a few minutes or hours after an individual treatment and up to several weeks after a series of treatments. Within three or four weeks after a series of treatments, most patients feel they have returned to their cognitive baseline. Some patients, however, have reported feeling foggy for up to several months after a complete series of ECT treatments.

Formal cognitive testing three months or more after a series of treatments have typically failed to show differences in memory between patients who have had ECT and those who have not. There are reports of some patients describing loss of selected important memories, such as memories of their wedding day; but this type of autobiographical memory loss appears to be uncommon. Post-ECT memory loss may be reduced by the use of unilateral rather than bilateral electrodes. Shorter total seizure duration is associated with reduced memory problems and reduced efficacy.

References:

American Psychiatric Association. Practice guidelines for major depressive disorder in adults. Washington, DC, APA Press, 1993.

American Psychiatric Association: The practice of ECT: Recommendations for treatment, training, and privileging. Convulsive Therapy 1990;6(2):85-120.

Fink M: Convulsive therapy: How it evolved. Psychopharm Bull 1986;22(2):457-459.

Jenike MA: Treatment of affective illness in the elderly with drugs and electroconvulsive therapy. J Geriat Psychiat 1989;22:77-112.

Kellner CH, Nixon DW, Bernstein HJ: ECT/drug interactions: A review. Psychopharm Bull 1991; 27(4):595-609.

Khan A, Mirolo MH, Hughes D, Bierut L: Electroconvulsive therapy. Psychiatr Clinics N Amer Sept 1993;16(3):497-513.

National Institute of Health, Consensus Conference: Electroconvulsive therapy. JAMA 1985; 254(15):2103-2108.

The Royal College of Psychiatrists: The Royal College of Psychiatrists memorandum on the use of electroconvulsive therapy. Br J Psychiatry 1977;131:261-272.

NOTES

#12 The Role of Psychotherapy

Despite the emphasis of this book on biological therapies of depression, psychotherapy continues to play an invaluable role in the treatment of depression. Psychotherapy may be defined as a process by which emotional and behavioral change is achieved through the verbal exchange of two or more people. It was not long ago that depression was defined in purely psychological terms and the treatment of choice was long-term psychotherapy. Neither purely psychological nor purely biological treatments appear to be adequate in all cases of major depression. Rather, the optimal therapy of depression may represent an integration of biological and psychological approaches.

Many forms of psychotherapy have been applied to the treatment of major depression, but relatively few have been well studied in terms of outcome. It would appear that many depressed patients are good candidates for psychotherapy, especially outpatients with mild to moderate depressive episodes. Patients with more severe forms of depression, such as psychotic depression, have generally not been regarded as suitable candidates for psychotherapy alone in the acute stage of the disorder.

Several types of psychotherapy have been studied and found to be effective, (see Table 12.1) including:

- Individual psychotherapies in which one trained therapist works with one patient
- Family therapy in which a therapist works with a couple or multiple family members
- Group psychotherapy in which a group of patients works with one or two co-leaders

Cognitive-Behavioral Therapy (CBT)

Cognitive-behavioral therapy is the single best-studied psychotherapy in the treatment of depression. It evolved from the work of Aaron T. Beck in the early 1960s as a specific treatment for major depression, but currently it is also employed in treating anxiety and other disorders.

CBT is based on the premise that negative perceptions and thoughts are not simply the result of a depressive episode but that these distorted thoughts and perceptions may cause or exacerbate depression. Studies have demonstrated that, in major depression, thought processes are characterized by a number of cognitive errors, thoughts that manifest a pattern of faulty reasoning. These thoughts occur often in depressed patients, including catastrophic thoughts in which patients ignore likely outcomes and dwell on the worst possible outcome. Depressed patients, for example, may make a minor error at the office and think that this error will cost them their careers or promotions when, in reality, the error is of no significance.

Another form of cognitive error is absolutist, or all-or-nothing, thinking, in which patients divide their experiences into rigid dichotomies. In this case, employees who make a minor error at the office conclude that they are bad employees, since good employees do not make such errors.

Other cognitive errors in depressed patients frequently are of an "automatic" quality; thoughts occur too rapidly for rational assessment, and patients are not fully aware of the extent of their occurrence. Automatic thoughts and cognitive errors are associated with emotional states, such as despair, anxiety, and a sense of hopelessness.

Among the principal goals of cognitive therapy are identifying and modifying negative automatic thoughts. Therapy is generally limited to 10 to 20 sessions, and homework is usually assigned between sessions. One common homework assignment, intended to help identify automatic thoughts early in treatment is thought recording, in which patients are assigned to keep a diary of automatic thoughts, the situations in which they occur, and their emotional reactions to them. In later sessions, the thoughts can be examined and challenged through evaluation of the basis for these cognitions and subsequent reframing of those situations.

In addition to the assessment and modification of distorted thoughts and perceptions, CBT has two other important components: education and behavioral aspects. Patients with major depression are provided educational material regarding the features and natural course of the disorder, may be referred to additional books and/or articles on the subject, and are provided discussion sessions early in therapy in which the nature of CBT is fully discussed and patients are encouraged to ask questions.

Behavioral aspect deals with the specific techniques used to mobilize the depressed patient and address problem areas. Cognitive behavioral therapists, for example, may employ social skills or assertiveness training in some patients, assign week-long schedules of activities for others who are frequently immobilized by their illness, and give step-by-step, or graded, task assignments to those who face tasks they perceive as overwhelming. Patients who procrastinate about getting their tax returns completed, for example, are adding to their anxiety and despair; they may be assigned just to sit at their desks and open the tax return on the first day, to review the tax return from last year on the second day, collect income statements for the current year on the third day, begin working on the forms on the fourth day, etc. This method leads patients to mastery over important tasks and subsequently enhances self-esteem.

Studies comparing CBT to pharmacotherapy for the treatment of depression have generally been favorable. For many patients, CBT may be as effective as treatment with medication and the techniques learned may reduce risks of relapse. Some studies suggest that CBT may be less effective in most severe forms of depression, while other studies have concluded that the combination of CBT and pharmacotherapy may be better than either treatment used alone.

Interpersonal Psychotherapy (IPT)

Interpersonal psychotherapy is another form of psychotherapy developed by Gerald Klerman and his colleagues specifically for the treatment of depression. It is based on the premise that depression mostly is the result of deficiencies in social functioning, intimacy, dependency, and isolation. Its efficacy in treating depression has been established by a number of studies.

IPT, like CBT, is usually limited to 10 to 20 therapy sessions. In the initial phase, a detailed symptom history is obtained, the nature of depression is discussed, and an inventory of significant current and past social relationships is reviewed.

Problem areas, such as interpersonal disputes or grief reactions to the loss of loved ones, also are identified.

Later sessions are devoted to clarifying negative feelings around interpersonal problems and identifying options for dealing with these problems. The focus is on patients' difficulties in current social relationships, rather than on cognition or general coping strategies. Important aspects include:

- Reassuring patients
- Legitimizing patients' sick roles
- Testing patients' perceptions
- Improving patients' interpersonal communications

IPT appears to enhance social functioning in depressed patients. Though it has not been as well studied as CBT, patients who are treated with IPT in combination with pharmacotherapy appear to have the best results.

Psychodynamic Therapy

Psychodynamic psychotherapy, based on the work of Sigmund Freud, has been used to treat depression and other problems since the turn of the century. Unfortunately, psychoanalytically oriented psychotherapy has not been subject to careful outcome studies, and its utility in the treatment of major depression has not been defined.

Psychoanalytic psychotherapy focuses on patients':

- Understanding unconscious motives and defenses as they relate to current conflicts
- Understanding difficulties in interpersonal relationships
- Working through on-going relationships

Generally, therapists take a less active and directive role in psychoanalytic therapy than with CBT or IPT, taking a reflective stance, except in supportive therapy, and rarely offering specific advise or directions.

Psychoanalytic psychotherapy has two predominate forms: insight-oriented therapy and supportive therapy. The goal of insight-oriented therapy is to help patients garner insight into the basis of their depressive episodes, understand the precipitating factors, and work through their feelings or maladaptive responses that may be exacerbating the depression. In psychoanalytic theory, the basis for depression is frequently understood in terms of a current loss, such as the loss of a loved one, but some losses may be more subtle, such as the loss of a fantasy that one would be successful by a certain age. Therapists may enhance patients' insight of loss by interpreting feelings and relating this loss to earlier ones in their lives. Ideally, by gaining insight, depressed patients are able to move beyond the sadness and get on with their lives.

The second form, supportive therapy, focuses less on obtaining insight and more on providing emotional support for patients as they contend with periods of illness or turmoil. For depressed patients, supportive psychotherapy is aimed at:

- Encouraging adequate rest
- Taking active steps to reduce current stresses
- Allowing patients to have a place to vent strong, unexpressed emotions

Psychodynamic therapy may be brief, lasting only 10 or 12 sessions, or open-ended, lasting two years or longer, with each session from 45 to 50 minutes and scheduled once or twice a week. This schedule is different from classical psychoanalysis sessions, which meet five days a week for several years.

Family Therapy

Among the environmental variables influencing the course of a depressive episode is patients' relationships with their families. Families can serve as buffers to protect patients from depression or may aggravate patients' vulnerability, and one member's struggle with major depressions may have a severe impact on family relationships, causing stressed relationships within the family and further exacerbating the depression. While family therapy is rarely used as the sole treatment for a depressive episode, it may be an important treatment option.

The goal of family therapy in treating depression is to improve family functioning while decreasing patients' depressive symptoms. This goal may be achieved by providing families with education about the course of depression, treatment options, and the disorder's impact on the lives of all concerned. Family therapy also focuses on developing family communication skills so that the all parties' needs are understood and met. Family therapy may also aid patients by limiting the effects and sense of isolation, focusing instead on enhancing family cohesion and encouraging a sense of connection not only between patients and their families but also with a wider

TABLE 12.1 — Comparison of Individual Psychotherapies of Depression

Type	Cognitive-Behavioral	Interpersonal	Psychodynamic
Premise	Depression secondary to cognitive distortion	Depression secondary to interpersonal problems	Depression secondary to unconscious conflict over a loss
Goal	Correct cognitive distortions	Enhance current social functioning	Resolve conflict over loss
Approach	Directive	Directive	Non-directive
Technique	Cognitive diary Homework assignments Graded tasks Assertiveness training	Reassurance Improve interpersonal communication Role rehearse interpersonal solutions	Interpret unconscious material Ventilation/catharsis Review historical basis of conflict
Duration	12 – 20 sessions	12 – 20 sessions	Brief (12 sessions) or open ended

Adapted from TB Karasu: Psychotherapy for depression. Am J Psychiatry 147;2:1990.

community of support.

Of the many formats for family therapy, the most common is for one therapist to meet with several family members in weekly, 50- to 120-minute sessions over the course of several months. Frequently, family therapy is concurrent with patients' individual treatments. Other formats include:

- Family group therapy, in which two or more families meet in the same group
- Conjoint therapy, in which two therapists of the opposite sex meet with two or more family members
- Multiple family groups brought together for a single, survival skills session, which:
  - Last four to six hours
  - Focuses on education about depression
  - Allows a sense of comfort and support from other families struggling with the depression of a family member

Whether or not formal family therapy is pursued, family involvement is often crucial, since families can be either allies or saboteurs to the treatment program. Meeting with families of depressed patients early in the course of treatment is invaluable in providing education about the rationale for a particular treatment plan, in obtaining additional history, and in enlisting family support in patient care.

Group Psychotherapy

Patients with major depression may derive substantial benefit from participation in group psychotherapy, in which patients are placed in a group, often with a particular focus, that is led by one or two trained therapists. All members of the group function, in a sense, as therapists for the other members. Thus, group patients may derive considerable support, validation, and insight from other group members. Group leaders facilitate the group process, assuring that all members are heard.

Depressed patients may be comforted by other patients having similar problems; the alliance and identification they develop may be therapeutic. Groups are ideal settings for patients' negative perceptions about themselves and their situations to be challenged; groups also may provide the encouragement—and pressure—patients need to become mobilized and increase their activity levels. Ideally, groups also serve as safe places for patients to ventilate strong emotions and have these feelings validated.

There are as many types of groups as there are individual therapies. Some are insight-oriented, while others have a cognitive-behavioral or supportive focus. Groups vary in size from as few as three patients to as many as 25, but eight to 10 is often ideal.

A typical therapy group meets once a week in 90-minute sessions. The therapy may be open-ended, lasting many years, or limited to 12 to 20 sessions.

Integrating Psychotherapy and Pharmacotherapy

Psychotherapy and pharmacotherapy are not mutually exclusive treatments for major depression but instead frequently complement each other.

A clinician's act of prescribing an antidepressant medication may have profound significance for patients, who may interpret the situation as meaning that they are sick, crazy, or unable to be helped by other treatments. Other patients, however, may be relieved when antidepressants are offered, since the act validates their sick role and relieves them of the idea that they are to blame for their problems. Still other patients may interpret a prescription to mean that they have a biological illness and that they, therefore, need not try to understand the psychological aspects of their depression. Integrating psychotherapy and medication management may provide clinicians with a greater understanding of the meaning of medications for patients and substantially increase the chance that patients will sustain a long antidepressant trial.

Likewise, medications may make it possible for psychotherapy to proceed, especially for those who are so anergic and compromised by their depressive episode that they cannot get out of bed, much less participate in psychotherapeutic relationships. Participating in psychotherapy requires that patients have enough energy and motivation to attend regularly scheduled visits and be able to concentrate at meetings. Antidepressants may mobilize these patients so that they may benefit from psychotherapy.

An increasingly common practice is to split treatment between physicians who prescribe medications and therapists (often psychologists, social workers, or counselors). There are advantages and disadvantages to this approach. One disadvantage is that splitting patient care may result in too many different ideas about optimal treatment approaches and a resultant undermining of both psychotherapy and pharmacotherapy.

Splitting care also may result in a diffusion of responsibility among caregivers so that no one person takes the role of principal clinician to coordinate care. Also, dividing the labor requires more work from clinicians who must compare notes and coordinate their efforts.

On the positive side, dividing treatment between prescribing physicians and psychotherapists may be particularly advantageous for complex patients who may benefit from the expertise of more than one professional. Another advantage may be that having a physician assigned to medication management may allow the psychotherapist to focus on the psychological work rather than on side effects of medications. Finally, there may be an economic advantage to dividing care; it may be less expensive for patients to see psychologists or counselors than psychiatrists, who handle both medication and psychotherapy but at higher costs. Nonetheless, psychiatrists who can personally coordinate patients' care may be optimal.

Some depressed patients will prefer to pursue psychotherapy alone. Others may consider psychotherapy a waste of time and agree only to being treated with antidepressant medications. Increasingly, economic factors determine the treatment course, since insurance carriers may only cover certain treatments. However, the integration of psychotherapy and pharmacotherapy may be the optimal treatment for many depressed patients.

References:

Anderson C: Family therapy for the depressed patient. In: Treating depression. Glick ID, ed. Jossey and Bass, San Francisco, in press, 1995.

Beck AT: Cognitive therapy of depression. Guilford Press, New York, 1979.

Beck AT: Depression: Causes and treatments. University of Pennsylvania Press, Philadelphia, PA, 1972.

Beitman BD, Klerman GL, eds.: Combining psychotherapy and drug therapy in clinical practice. Spectrum Publications, New York, 1984.

DiMascio A, Weissman MM: Treatment of Depression by Drugs and Psychotherapy. Am J of Psychiatry. 1974;131:186-191.

Klerman GL, Weissman MM, Rounsaville BJ, Chevron RS: Interpersonal psychotherapy of depression. Basic Books, Inc., New York, 1984.

Minuchin S: Families and family therapy. Harvard University Press. Cambridge, MA, 1974.

Strupp HH, Binder JL: Psychotherapy in a new key: A guide to time-limited dynamic psychotherapy. Basic Books, Inc., New York, 1984.

Yalom I: The theory and practice of group psychotherapy. Basic Books, Inc., New York, 3rd ed., 1985.

NOTES

#13 The Suicidal Patient

Suicide is the most serious and all too common outcome for a major depressive episode. Approximately 15 percent, or one in seven patients, with untreated or inadequately treated major depression ultimately take their own lives. Approximately 30,000 people per year commit suicide, representing a mortality rate of about 13 suicide deaths per 100,000 people in the U.S. Suicide attempts are at least eight times more common than completed suicides, and many deaths ruled to be accidental are probably suicides.

Available data suggest that all patients with major depression are at greater risk than the general population for committing suicide. However, determining the degree of risk for a given depressed patient is not a simple task. A thorough evaluation will help to determine whether a depressed patient needs to be detained involuntarily and admitted to a locked psychiatric unit or whether outpatient follow-up will suffice.

Assessing the Risk of Suicide

A number of risk factors in depressed patients can suggest that the situation is desperate and requires immediate attention. Perhaps the most important factor is patients' stated intentions. All depressed patients should be asked about suicidal thoughts and plans. The more time a patient spends dwelling on death or suicidal thoughts, the more worrisome the patient is, since patients with a specific, viable plan for suicide are among the most likely to succeed. These depressed patients not only have spent considerable time reviewing suicide options but also have addressed the aftermath of their demise. It is extremely ominous, for example, for depressed patients to begin giving away their cherished possessions or rewrite their wills for no apparent reason. Such patients generally need to be observed and require intense treatment in a secure inpatient setting. Other indications for increased suicide risk include (see Table 13.1):

- An oppressive sense of hopelessness
- The presence of panic symptoms
- A history of previous suicide attempts

Among the most important risk factors is a patient's age. The elderly have the highest rates of completed suicides of all age groups, with geriatric males almost four times more likely to succeed in their attempts than younger age groups.

Alcoholism is also implicated in many completed suicides. After major depression, alcoholism is the second most common disorder associated with suicide, at a rate 50 times greater than for the general population. In fact, 50 to 75 percent of all successful suicides appear to be related to depression, alcoholism, or both; the presence of alcoholism concurrently with major depression is common and may substantially increase the risk of a successful attempt, since the alcohol may be disinhibiting enough to allow patients to commit an action they might not otherwise pursue.

Gender is also important in assessing suicide risk. Females are at least twice as likely to attempt suicide as males; they account for 70 percent of all suicide attempts. Males, however, tend to use more lethal means of suicide, particularly guns; they are three times more likely to succeed in their attempts than females. Drug overdose is the most common means of attempting suicide.

Generally, patients who are not socially connected are at increased risk for both attempting and succeeding in suicide. Patients who are isolated, live alone, and lack good social support systems of friends and families pose a significant risk in the context of a major depressive episode. Conversely, patients who are married, have dependent children, and adequate social networks are at somewhat reduced risk.

Recently, severe anxiety and panic attacks also have been shown to be correlated with increased acute risk of suicide in depressed patients. Patients with severe anxiety symptoms may feel more overwhelmed and out of control than those without prominent anxiety, and global insomnia secondary to severe anxiety and depression also appears to increase the potential for suicide. Persistent lack of adequate sleep appears to exacerbate the dysphoria and, subsequently, the suicide risk. Likewise, obsessive-compulsive features in depressed patients may increase the short-term risk of suicide.

Some cognitive difficulties, such as diminished concentration and indecision, are common in major depression and appear to be correlated with an acute suicide risk. Patients who feel that their mental faculties are severely compromised may be less effective at problem solving and coping with their depression and may develop a sense of hopelessness that further increases the risk.

Finally, certain aspects of patients' histories may indicate an enhanced acute risk, especially a history of suicide attempts; and patients who have made near-lethal attempts are at obvious risk for making other attempts in the context of a major depressive episode. Patients with recurrent major depression also are at greater risk for attempting suicide, as are those with an absence of friends in adolescence, which may reveal a general lack of social "connectedness."

TABLE 13.1 – **Important Risk Factors for Suicide in Patients with Major Depression**
Acute alcohol abuse
History of recurrent depression, suicide attempts, lack of friends in adolescence
Male
Obsessive features
Over age 45
Severe anxiety or panic attacks
Severe cognitive difficulties; indecision and difficulty concentrating
Severe insomnia
Severe hopelessness
Viable suicide plan
(Adapted from Fawcett et al, 1990; Bongar 1992)

The Causes of Suicidal Behavior

Suicidal behavior may best be understood in both biological and psychological terms. Among the more popular early psychological theories of suicide have been those of Sigmund Freud and Karl Menninger. Freud saw depression and suicide as manifestations of what he understood to be anger turned inward and suggested that this anger typically arises from losing a "love object" (whether death of a loved one or of a friendship). Since this anger cannot be safely or practically directed to the loved one, it is directed to the self in suicidal patients.

Menninger extended Freud's theory by suggesting that suicide represents "inverted homicide" directed to the lost relationship and intended as a means of atonement for perceived sins. In this case, suicide may represent patients' deserved punishment for alienating important components of their social networks or failing in some aspect of their lives.

Recently, increasing evidence for a biological basis for some suicidal behavior has emerged. Identical twins, for example, appear to have a higher concordance rate for suicide even if they are reared separately from one another, which may suggest an underlying predisposition for disorders, such as depression or alcoholism, that increase suicide risk.

Several chemicals also appear to be correlated with an enhanced risk. Low cerebrospinal fluid levels of 5-hydroxyindoleacetic acid (5-HIAA), the major metabolite of serotonin, appear to be correlated with increased risks of suicidal behavior. Just as depression may be related to abnormalities in the serotonin system, it has been speculated that suicidal behavior may be directly correlated to significantly lower levels of serotonin in the brain.

Levels of cortisol, a stress hormone, may provide an estimate of patients' distress and arousal levels; elevated cortisol levels are frequently seen in patients with depression and other psychological disorders. Several studies suggest that higher cortisol levels may be correlated with a higher risk for suicide. Likewise, patients with elevated levels of corticosteroids in the urine also appear to be more vulnerable to suicidal behavior.

While the biological correlates of suicide remain an active area of research, biological factors have limited clinical implications at this time. Chemicals, such as 5-HIAA, are difficult to measure and are not specific or sensitive enough to have much predictive value in clinical assessment of potentially suicidal patients. However, research will continue in an attempt to understand the biological underpinnings of suicidal behavior.

The Management of a Potentially Suicidal Depressed Patient

Reliably predicting the risk of suicide in depressed patients is often difficult. As a general rule, it is advisable for clinicians to err on the side of safety and hospitalize patients who appear to be acutely suicidal. Sometimes the decision to hospitalize patients against their will is an easy one; for example, hospitalization on a secure psychiatric unit is the clear disposition for a patient who shows up in an emergency room after making a serious suicide attempt. Likewise, patients with histories of suicide attempts who appear hopeless and depressed and voice a plan for suicide should be hospitalized. Of course, many situations are less clear.

Patients evaluated in emergency rooms and assessed to be at acute suicide risk should be hospitalized, against their will if necessary. Most counties provide emergency room physicians with the legal power to detain patients if probable cause (evidence based on clinical history and presentation that patients are at some acute risk for harming themselves) exists. Even if patients are willing to go to a hospital, it is sometimes advisable for physicians to place them on legal hold as a danger to themselves so these patients may be observed and further assessed for 72 hours in a secure psychiatric facility.

A more difficult situation occurs when suicidal patients call from home or another setting. It is impossible for clinicians adequately to assess these patients over the phone. If patients are able to come to an office or emergency room, they should be instructed to do so. If they are unwilling or unable to do so, clinicians should request assistance through 911 emergency telephone services. The police or other emergency personnel will check on patients' well being and bring them to emergency rooms for evaluation if it is determined that they are at risk for harming themselves.

Occasionally, suicidal patients may be managed on an outpatient basis if they:

- Have no history of prior suicide attempts
- Can and will "contract" not to harm themselves
- Have family and social support that allows for their close observation
- Can be followed with close outpatient psychiatric care

If there is any question about whether patients can control their suicidal impulses, however, psychiatric hospitalization is indicated.

Whether potentially suicidal patients are treated on inpatient or outpatient bases, it is crucial that psychiatric consultation is obtained. Management of suicidal patients is a life and death issue, and consultations should be sought from specialists most experienced at dealing with such patients.

Clinicians use several principles in treating suicidal patients besides keeping them safe from themselves. The first is reducing the real psychological pain and distress being experienced. This can be done through psychotherapy, social interventions, and medications. Depressed, suicidal patients feel miserable and almost uniformly do not believe that anything can help them. The acute use of benzodiazepines, such as lorazepam (Ativan), to help mitigate anxiety and insomnia can be tremendously useful in helping patients feel better rapidly. At the same time, educating patients about the nature of depression, reassuring them that they can feel much better than they do, and starting treatment with antidepressant medications may be important. In addition, electroconvulsive therapy used to treat an imminently suicidal depressed patient has been lifesaving in many cases.

Offering patients an alternative to suicide is another treatment principle. Depressed patients often feel trapped by their overwhelming emotional states and come to the conclusion that suicide is the most viable option or only logical solution to their problems. Cognitive behavioral therapists examine the advantages and disadvantages of suicide with patients, while examining, too, their faulty evidence that suicide is the best option available.

Just as depression is a treatable problem in most cases, so is suicidal ideation and behavior.

To be treated effectively, however, suicidal patients must be first identified. Suicidal patients often present to their primary care physicians with vague expressions of "giving up." Unfortunately these expressions of hopelessness are often dismissed. It is only after identifying the suicidal patient that biological and psychosocial interventions can be brought to bear.

References:

Bongar B: Suicide: Guidelines for assessment, management and treatment. Oxford Press, New York, 1992.

Clayton PJ: Suicide. Psychiatric Clinics of North America 1985;8:203-214.

Cullberg J, Wasserman D, Sefansson CG: Who commits suicide after a suicide attempt? Acta Pychiatrica Scand 1988;77:598-603.

Fawcett J, Scheftner WA, Clark DC: Time-related predictors of suicide. Am J Psychiatry 1990;147: 1189-1194.

Frankel F: The use of electroconvulsive therapy in suicidal patients. M J Psychotherapy 1984;38:384-391.

Motto J: Clinical considerations of biological correlates of suicide. Suicide and Life Threatening Behavior 1986;16:83-102.

Murphy GE: Clinical identification of suicide risk. Arch Gen Psychiatry 1972;27:356-359.

Murphy GE, Wetzel RD: The lifetime risk of suicide in alcoholism. Arch Gen Psychiatry 1990;47:383-392.

Roy A: Suicide. Williams and Wilkins, Baltimore, 1986.

Slaby AE, Tancredi LR: The handbook of psychiatric emergencies. Elsevier Press, New York. 4th ed., 1991.

#14 Geriatric and Pediatric Depression

The vast majority of studies on the treatment of depression, particularly antidepressant studies, have excluded patients below age 18 and over age 65, yet people on each end of the age spectrum constitute a significant percentage of patients with major depressive episodes.

Geriatric and pediatric patients frequently have different clinical presentations of depression than patients in other age groups, and these patients may not respond to or tolerate treatments in the same manner as other age groups. Therefore, assessment and treatment of geriatric and pediatric depression are considered separately in this section.

GERIATRIC DEPRESSION

Although elderly patients (over age 65) constitute only 11 percent of the population, they constitute 20 percent of all patients who commit suicide. In some settings, such as nursing homes, up to 33 percent of patients meet criteria for major depression. Thus, the elderly are among the most vulnerable age groups for developing major depression and for its having a lethal outcome. Furthermore, geriatric patients are susceptible to problems that may be related to depression, such as grief and dementia.

Causes

Causes of depression in the elderly appear to overlap those in other age groups. Biological factors that appear to be important in geriatric depression include:

- Age-related decreases in monoamine neurotransmitters
- Reduced cerebral blood flow
- Decreased oxidative metabolism, necessary for production and metabolism of neurotransmitters in the brain

Psychosocial stresses are also significant factors in the onset of depression in geriatric patients. The elderly, for example, are most at risk for losing loved ones, especially spouses. Few losses in life equal the loss of a life partner, and those geriatric patients with a vulnerability to major depression often develop a depressive episode over such a loss. In addition, aging is associated with other major losses, such as loss of identity, including loss of vocational role; as patients retire from their lives' work, they may lose an important sense of purpose, significant parts of their social support systems, and financial security. The combination of psychosocial losses and age-related compromises in biological integrity appear to enhance the risk of depression in the elderly.

The frequency of complicating medical factors, especially concurrent medications, needs careful assessment in the elderly. The elderly are more likely than any other age group to take multiple medications, including antihypertensives, sedatives, and exogenous hormones, that may contribute to depressive symptoms. In addition, the elderly are at most risk for underlying medical disorders, including malignancies, neurological disorders, and endocrine abnormalities, that may present with depression.

Assessment

The frequency of confounding medical problems in geriatric depressed patients requires careful review of systems, general physical and neurological examinations, and laboratory studies. Geriatric depression often presents with "masked" symptoms, including numerous somatic complaints that require assessment, and can distract clinicians from considering underlying depression as the diagnosis. Somatic complaints in all age groups may represent a more socially acceptable way of expressing pain, including psychological suffering.

Dementia is sometimes clinically confused with depression in the elderly, since depressed patients frequently have cognitive difficulties, referred to as "pseudodementia" and demented patients may appear depressed. What distinguishes demented from depressed patients is usually their histories. Demented patients usually have a history of slow, insidious progression to their memory loss, are disoriented, and may have related difficulties, such as incontinence. Depressed patients, on the other hand, may have a rapid onset to their cognitive problems, remain oriented, and have related depressive effects, including agitation and irritability. Furthermore, cognitive difficulties in depressed patients will be more erratic than those in demented patients; depressed patients may appear more impaired at times than others and respond to questions with "I don't know" rather than give the near-miss answers of demented patients.

Depression also is often confused with grief in the elderly. In general, patients with grief reactions (see Section #2) persisting longer than two months or accompanied by symptoms, such as suicidal ideation or psychomotor retardation, should be considered for antidepressant therapy.

Treatment

Mild depressive episodes in the elderly frequently respond to individual psychotherapy, with the cognitive-behavioral therapy (CBT) type being the best studied in the treatment of geriatric patients. Patients often have significant relief from their depressive symptoms in the first three months of treatment.

For severe depressive episodes, ECT or pharmacotherapy is generally indicated in elderly patients. Despite its risks, ECT may be better tolerated than many antidepressant medications in geriatric patients, is more likely to be effective, and is quicker acting than medication trials. For these reasons, some clinicians advise using ECT sooner rather than later in treating depressed geriatric patients.

Pharmacotherapy of geriatric depression is complicated by an increased risk of side effects for all antidepressants, related, in part, to age-induced reductions in hepatic metabolism and renal clearance. Thus, elderly patients frequently require lower doses of antidepressants than those required in younger age groups. A common practice in pharmacotherapy of geriatric patients is to initiate treatment at half the recommended starting dose and titrate the medication up to half the usual maximum dose, as tolerated.

Antidepressants in the elderly are chosen mostly by side effect profile. In general, anticholinergic antidepressants, such as amitriptyline (Elavil), are poorly tolerated in these patients and should be avoided. Geriatric patients are at greater risk than other populations for developing confusion, urinary retention, and constipation on anticholinergic antidepressants. Also, drugs that may lower blood pressure substantially, including MAOIs and trazodone (Desyrel), must be used with caution. Among the most popular SSRIs for treating geriatric patients is sertraline (Zoloft) because of its short half-life, limited side effects, and limited risk of interacting with other medications. Among the cyclic drugs, nortriptyline (Pamelor) is a fair choice, given its limited anticholinergic effects and long track record in treating geriatric depression. Other reasonable choices include bupropion (Wellbutrin) and venlafaxine (Effexor).

TABLE 14.1 – **Pharmacotherapy in Geriatric Depression**

Favorable Drugs	**Less Favorable Drugs**
Sertraline (Zoloft)	Amitriptyline (Elavil)
Nortriptyline (Pamelor)	Doxepin (Sinequan)
Bupropion (Wellbutrin)	Phenelzine (Nardil)
Venlafaxine (Effexor)	Tranylcypromine (Parnate)
Nefazodone (Serzone)	Imipramine (Tofranil)

PEDIATRIC DEPRESSION

Pediatric depression has been the focus of increasing research during the past 25 years. Prior to that time, many mental health professionals doubted the existence of depression in children, but it has become increasingly evident that pediatric depression is not uncommon.

Depression in pre-pubescent children is estimated at approximately two percent. By adolescence, the prevalence more than doubles to about five percent. In addition, the rate of adolescent suicide is increasing; since 1957, the suicide rate in the 15- to 19-year-old age bracket has quadrupled, with the current rate of 11.3 per 100,000 higher than that for the 21- to 55-year-old age group and considerably lower than that for the geriatric population. Thus, pediatric depression is associated with significant mortality, and the mood disorder often continues into adulthood.

Causes

The causes of childhood depression are less well studied than those of adult depression; but, as with depression in other age groups, pediatric depression may be associated with certain medications, including antihypertensives, phenobarbital, and steroids. In addition, children with certain chronic illnesses, such as epilepsy and juvenile diabetes, appear to have a greater vulnerability for developing major depression.

Biological factors in childhood appear to be important to increased risks of depression. Neuroendocrine studies suggest that depressed children differ from normal controls in having a blunted prolactin response to 5-HT_2, an abnormality that may suggest a deficit in noradrenergic and serotonergic neurotransmission.

Perhaps the biggest risk factor for children developing a major depressive episode is their having a parent who is affectively ill. Depression in one parent may increase the possibility of the genetic transmission of depression to a child; a depressed parent's emotional isolation may also enhance risk. Having one parent with depression may double the risk that a child will suffer from depression; having both parents affected appears to increase the risk by four to five times. As with depression in other age groups, pediatric depression also may result from a loss of some kind.

Assessment

The DSM IV criteria for diagnosing a major depressive episode in children is the same that is employed for adults, with two exceptions. One is that depressed children and adolescents may sometimes present with irritable as opposed to depressed mood. Children may not endorse "feeling sad" and should be asked about feeling mad, bored, down, or just not good inside. Conduct disorders sometimes also occur secondary to depression in children and adolescents; thus, pediatric depression may present with a new onset of behavior problems. In adolescents, alcohol and illicit drug use may be the presenting problem. School performance is frequently compromised during a major depressive episode and may present clues to underlying difficulties with motivation, interest, and concentration.

The second difference in the DSM IV criteria for diagnosing major depression in children is that the weight changes seen in depressed adults may present in children as a failure to achieve expected weight gains. Thus, the large differential diagnosis in children who indicate a drop on growth weight charts should include severe depression. Failure to achieve expected weight gains in a major depressive episode will always be accompanied by other symptoms of depression, such loss of energy, interest, motivation, and cognitive ability; however, depression is frequently overlooked by pediatricians as a possible factor in pre-pubescent children's sudden difficulties with growth.

Treatment

Treatment of pediatric depression requires consultation with experienced mental health professionals. Medication management and psychotherapy parallel but do not replicate the results of those treatments for adult patients.

There are few controlled studies on efficacy of antidepressants in children and adolescents, since children under age 18 are typically excluded from major clinical drug trials. Of the few independent studies conducted for treatment with MAOIs, tricyclics, and fluoxetine (Prozac), there is no convincing evidence that antidepressants are superior to placebo in children. This lack of response is difficult to interpret, given that the studies have generally been small and that pediatric patients metabolize many of these drugs differently than adults do. For example, pre-pubescent children metabolize tricyclic drugs more rapidly than adults, since their livers are larger relative to the rest of their bodies; these may be factors in the rapid metabolism of some antidepressants. Thus, on a milligram-of-drug-per-kilogram-of-weight basis, children may require larger doses of antidepressants to obtain adequate responses.

Unfortunately, children also have lower body fat-to-muscle ratios, which decrease the volume of distribution of fat-soluble drugs and may increase children's vulnerability to the toxic effects of some antidepressants.

Despite the lack of overwhelming evidence that antidepressants are effective in children, some pediatric patients clearly do better on medication treatment. Thus, antidepressants may be considered for children with depressive episodes that:

- Do not improve spontaneously
- Are associated with significant impairment in functioning
- Are associated with a significant risk of suicide

Tricyclic drugs have been the most studied antidepressants for treating pediatric depression. One precaution before starting tricyclic treatment in children is to obtain an EKG to rule out a latent conduction defect. TCAs have been rarely associated with sudden deaths in children, and the presumed cause is malignant arrhythmias. Such arrhythmias may occur in the context of an underlying conduction defect, such as a second-degree heart block. Thus, even children should be subject to a screening 12-lead EKG before TCAs are prescribed.

Tricyclics are typically prescribed on a mg-per-kg basis for children. Most tricyclic drugs, such as amitriptyline (Elavil), desipramine (Norpramin), and imipramine (Tofranil), are initiated at a dose of 1.5 mg per kg per day and are often increased by a maximum of 1 mg per kg per day every four days to a maximum of 5 mg per kg per day (see Table 14.2). The dose probably should not be given at one time as is common in treating adults but should be split in two or three divided doses. Nortriptyline (Pamelor) is prescribed in doses starting at 0.5 mg per kg per day to a maximum of 2 mg per kg per day. Obtaining

TABLE 14.2 — **Some Antidepressants Used to Treat Pediatric Depression**

Drug	Starting Dose	Maximum Dose	Plasma Levels
Amitriptyline (Elavil)	1 mg/kg/day	5 mg/kg/day	150-250 ng/ml
Bupropion (Wellbutrin)	1 mg/kg/day	5 mg/kg/day	– none –
Desipramine (Norpramin)	1 mg/kg/day	5 mg/kg/day	150-250 ng/ml
Fluoxetine (Prozac)	5 mg/day	20-30 mg/day	– none –
Imipramine (Tofranil)	1 mg/kg/day	5 mg/kg/day	150-250 ng/ml
Nortriptyline (Pamelor)	0.5 mg/kg/day	2 mg/kg/day	75-150 ng/ml

plasma levels of tricyclics in children may be important in predicting response and toxicity.

Other drugs used to treat pediatric depression patients include:

- Bupropion (Wellbutrin)
- Fluoxetine (Prozac)
- MAOIs

While some case reports suggest that these drugs may be useful in some children, further study is needed.

Augmentation strategies are also poorly studied in children. Lithium augmentation may be of benefit in some cases of treatment-resistant adolescent depression, but the findings are inconsistent. Other augmentation strategies have not been studied.

Most forms of psychotherapy that have been useful in treating depressed adults have been modified and applied to treatments for children and adolescents. Modified forms of interpersonal (IPT) and cognitive-behavioral therapy (CBT) may be useful. In addition, family therapy is often important in the successful treatment of these patients. Familial crises may precipitate and be precipitated by pediatric depression in a family member. Understanding the family dynamics may provide insights useful to treatment approaches. Any treatment plan that does not involve the family or caretakers is vulnerable to failure for this population of depressed patients.

References:

Bergener M: Geropsychiatric diagnostics and treatment. Springer, New York, 1983.

Brent DA: Depression and suicide in children and adolescents. Pediatrics in Review 1993;14(10):380-388.

Brent DA, Kolko DJ: The assessment and treatment of children and adolescents at risk for suicide. In: Suicide over the life cycle: Risk factors, assessment, and treatment of suicidal patients. Blumenthal SJ, Kupfer DJ, eds. APA Press, Washington, DC, 1990.

Brock CD, Simpson WM: Dementia, depression, or grief? The differential diagnosis. Geriatrics 45(10):37-43.

Cantwell DP, Carlson GA, eds.: Affective disorders in childhood and adolescence: An update. Spectrum Publications, New York, 1983.

Greenblatt DJ, Abernathy DR, Shader RI: Pharmacokinetic aspects of drug therapy in the elderly: Therapeutic drug monitoring. 1986;8:249.

Kovacs M, Feinberg T, Crouse-Novak M et al.: Depressive disorders in childhood. 1. A longitudinal prospective study of characteristics and recovery. Ach Gen Psychiatry 1984;41:221-237.

Plotkin DA, Gershon SC, Jarvik LF, Meltzer HY: Antidepressant drug treatment in the elderly. In: Psychopharmacology: Third generation of progress. Raven Press, New York, 1987.

Ryan ND: Pharmacological treatment of child and adolescent major depression. L'Encephale 1993;19:67-70.

Wilkes TC, Rush AJ: Adaptation of cognitive therapy for depressed adolescents. J Am Acad Child Adolescent Psychiatry 1988;27:381-386.

Yesavage JA: Depression in the elderly: How to recognize masked symptoms and choose appropriate therapy. Postgraduate Medicine 1990;91 (1):255-261.

NOTES

#15 Treating Depression by Subtype

It has become increasingly clear for the past 30 years that major depression is not a single illness but encompasses a number of disorders that may have distinct causes and may respond to different treatments. Several subtypes of major depression, described in the *Diagnostic and Statistical Manual of Mental Disorders (DSM IV)*, may respond better to some treatment regimens than others. These subtypes include:

- Psychotic depression
- Melancholic depression
- Atypical depression
- Seasonal affective disorder

Psychotic Depression

Psychotic depression is characterized by hallucinations or delusions in the context of a major depressive episode. The psychotic symptoms often are congruent with depressed mood; for example, psychotically depressed patients may have delusions that they bear responsibility and blame for some event in the past that they had little to do with, such as the death of a loved one. Sometimes, psychotically depressed patients experience auditory hallucinations that tell them they are worthless and that there is no hope that things will ever get better. If psychotic symptoms do not involve thoughts of death, guilt, disease, or personal inadequacy, they are said to be mood-incongruent (i.e., a delusion that men from Mars are invading the earth). Psychotic depression is not listed in the DSM IV as a distinct subtype of depression but is considered a severe form of major depression (see Figure 15.1 and Table

FIGURE 15.1 – Algorithm for the Treatment of Major Depression Subtypes

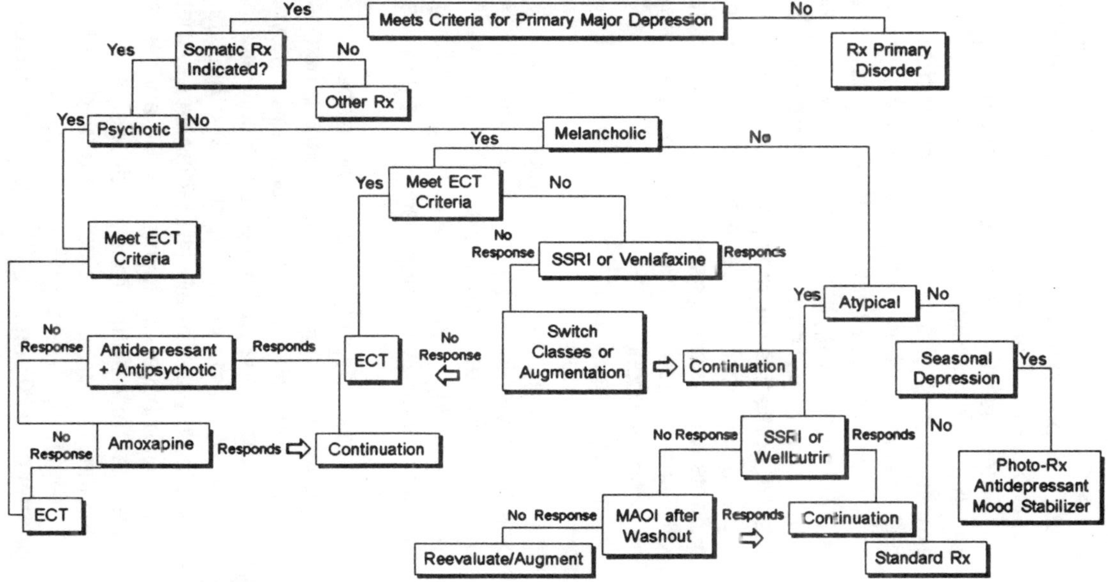

15.1). Nonetheless, psychotic depression appears to have a treatment response different from that of depression and is not characterized by delusions or hallucinations.

Some investigators have suggested that the psychosis in psychotic depression is driven by excessive cortisol, a stress hormone, and that the depression is often characterized by a hypercortisolemic state. Psychotic depressions may be characterized by higher levels of cortisol and adrenal activity than other forms of depression. Excessive cortisol levels may predispose some patients to psychosis in the same manner that some patients with Cushing's disease or those treated with large doses of glucocorticoids sometimes become psychotic.

It is believed that the elevated cortisol levels may drive the dopamine system into over-activity and that this, in turn, may be responsible for the psychotic symptoms. The adrenal hyperactivity in psychotic depression may also be responsible for the particularly high rates of nonsuppression on the dexamethasone suppression test (see Section #3).

Psychotic depression does not appear to respond well to antidepressants alone. When psychotic depression has been treated with tricyclic agents alone, the response rate is only half that seen in major depressive patients without psychotic features. Virtually all studies on psychotic depression have employed tricyclic antidepressant. When antipsychotic drugs, such as perphenazine or haloperidol, are added to a tricyclic regimen, the response rate is sometimes greater than 70 percent. Thus, psychotic depression appears to be less likely to respond to

TABLE 15.1 — **DSM IV Criteria for Severity of a Major Depressive Episode**

Mild Without Psychotic Features	
Moderate Without Psychotic Features	
Severe Without Psychotic Features	
Severe With Psychotic Features	Delusions or hallucinations. If possible, specify whether psychotic features are mood-congruent or mood-incongruent.
Mood-Congruent Psychotic Features	Delusions or hallucinations whose content is entirely consistent with depressive themes of personal inadequacy, guilt, disease, death, nihilism, or deserved punishment.
Mood-Incongruent Psychotic Features	Delusions or hallucinations whose content does not involve typical depressive themes of personal adequacy, guilt, disease, death, nihilism, or deserved punishment. Included are such symptoms as persecutory delusions (not directly related to depressive themes), thought insertion, thought broadcasting, and delusions of control.

(Reprinted with permission of publisher)

monotherapy with antidepressant treatment alone than does non-psychotic depression.

An exception to the idea that psychotic depression does not respond to monotherapy may be amoxapine (Asendin), a tetracyclic antidepressant chemically related to the antipsychotic drug loxapine. At least one careful study suggests that amoxapine is as effective alone as a combination of tricyclic antidepressants and antipsychotic drugs in treating psychotic depression.

As described earlier, electroconvulsive therapy (ECT) may be the treatment of choice for psychotic depression. Most studies suggest that ECT appears to be superior to antidepressant treatment and may act more quickly. Even with adequate and aggressive treatment, complete remission of symptoms may still require several months.

Several treatment strategies are possible. It is reasonable for clinicians to initiate a combination of antidepressant and antipsychotic drug treatment or, if patients meet the criteria, to commence ECT. Any patient with a psychotic depression that is life-threatening, is characterized by catatonia, or for which drug therapy has been unsuccessful or is not tolerated should be considered for ECT (see Table 11.1).

A tricyclic antidepressant with doses in the 150 to 300 mg per day range equivalent to imipramine (Tofranil) may be employed. Alternatively, fluoxetine (Prozac) has been used in doses of 20 to 60 mg per day, but it is not nearly as well studied in the treatment of psychotic depression as the tricyclic drugs. In addition, an antipsychotic, such as perphenazine, can be started simultaneously and will ultimately require doses of 30 to

60 mg per day. Combination treatment should continue for six to 12 weeks.

If combination therapy is not successful, a trial of amoxapine (Asendin) may be warranted. Amoxapine has been studied as sole therapy for psychotic depression with doses in the 200 to 400 mg per day range. Failure to respond to a second medication trial with amoxapine warrants a trial of ECT.

Melancholic Depression

The diagnosis of melancholia dates back many years and most recently has referred to a severe type of major depression presumed to be biologically driven and particularly responsive to somatic interventions. In DSM IV, the diagnosis of melancholia refers primarily to a major depressive episode with severe anhedonia or a loss of mood reactivity and prominent neurovegetative symptoms (see Table 15.2).

Despite the historical concept of melancholia as a type of depression that is responsive to biological treatments, it has been difficult to prove that it is more responsive to antidepressants or ECT than any other type of depression. However, there is some mixed evidence that melancholic depression may be less responsive to placebo, hospitalization alone, and psychotherapy alone than non-melancholic major depression.

Most studies have employed MAOIs and tricyclic antidepressants. However, several recent studies suggest that SSRIs and venlafaxine (Effexor) are also useful in treating melancholic inpatients. Some investigators do not believe the SSRIs are as effective for treating melancholic depression as are the TCAs. Nonetheless, given

TABLE 15.2 — **DSM IV Criteria for Melancholic Features**

A. Either of the following, occurring during the most severe period of the current episode:
   (1) Loss of pleasure in all, or almost all, activities
   (2) Lack of reactivity to usually pleasurable stimuli (does not feel much better, even temporarily, when something good happens)

B. Three (or more) of the following:
   (1) Distinct quality of depressed mood (i.e., the depressed mood is experienced as distinctly different from the kind of feelings experienced after the death of a loved one)
   (2) Depression regularly worse in the morning
   (3) Early morning awakenings (at least two hours before usual time of awakening)
   (4) Marked psychomotor retardation or agitation
   (5) Significant anorexia or weight loss
   (6) Excessive or inappropriate guilt

the more benign side effect profile of the newer drugs, it may be reasonable for treatment to be initiated with SSRIs or venlafaxine (Effexor). Typically, the doses are at the higher end of the therapeutic range. For example, many melancholic patients appear to require the maximum dose of 375 mg per day of venlafaxine and 50 mg per day of paroxetine (Paxil). If no response is seen after four to eight weeks at maximum doses, augmentation with lithium or switching to cyclic antidepressants or MAOIs may be attempted after adequate washout. Failure of two adequate trials of antidepressants warrants consideration of ECT.

Atypical Depression

The term atypical depression was first used to describe patients who responded preferentially to MAOIs and has meant different things to different investigators. It is included in the DSM IV criteria to describe patients who maintain an ability to respond positively to valued activities or events (mood reactivity) while having "reverse" neurovegetative symptoms. Instead of anorexia and insomnia, atypical depression is characterized by weight gain and hypersomnia. In addition, patients with atypical depression may complain of a heavy feeling in their limbs and may commonly have histories of heightened sensitivity to any interpersonal rejection (see Table 15.3).

During the past 30 years, studies have rather consistently demonstrated that patients with atypical depression respond preferentially to MAOIs rather than cyclic antidepressants. No studies have compared MAOIs with the newer agents; however, both fluoxetine (Prozac) and bupropion (Wellbutrin) have shown promise in treating atypical depression.

TABLE 15.3 — DSM IV Criteria for Atypical Features

A. Mood reactivity (i.e., mood brightens in response to actual or potential positive events)

B. Two (or more) of the following:
   1. Significant weight gain or increase in appetite
   2. Hypersomnia
   3. Leaden paralysis (i.e., heavy, leaden feelings in arms or legs)
   4. Long-standing pattern of interpersonal rejection sensitivity (not limited to episodes of a mood disturbance that results in significant social or occupational impairment).

C. Criteria are not met with *melancholic* or *catatonic features* during the same episode.

A reasonable strategy for treating atypical depression may be to initiate treatment with bupropion or SSRIs. While MAOIs have a more substantial track record, they also are more potentially problematic. Therefore, most clinicians no longer employ MAOIs as first-line treatment, even for atypical depression. However, if either bupropion or SSRIs are unsuccessful at inducing remission, either attempting augmentation or switching to MAOIs is warranted. Phenelzine (Nardil) started at 30 mg per day and increased to a maximum of 1 mg per kg is typically employed.

ECT is rarely used in treating atypical depression. There is no substantial evidence that it offers advantages over other treatments.

Seasonal Affective Disorder

It has been understood for many years that there is a seasonal pattern to some patients' depression. Usually, these patients complain that they begin to feel depressed in the fall as the days begin to shorten, that by winter they are quite depressed, and that they often come out of the depression as the days lengthen in the spring. For many, the disorder is limited to winter depressions; for others, a seasonal bipolar pattern is present, with periods of hypomania or mania in the spring and summer. In general, seasonal affective disorder describes a group of mood disorders with a distinct seasonal pattern (see Table 15.4).

Like other subtypes of major depression, seasonal depressions may respond better to some interventions than others. Given the temporal relationship of the depressive episodes to the seasons, it has been speculated that mood disorders may be directly related to quantity of daylight

TABLE 15.4 — **DSM IV Criteria for Seasonal Pattern**

A. A regular temporal relationship between the onset of major depressive episodes in bipolar I or bipolar II disorder or major depressive disorder, recurrent, occurs at a particular time of the year (e.g., regular winter appearance of the major depressive episode in the fall or winter). **Note:** Do not include cases in which there is an obvious effect of seasonal-related psychosocial stressors (e.g., regularly being unemployed every winter).

B. Full remission or a change from depression to mania or hypomania also occurs at a characteristic time of the year (e.g., depression disappears in the spring).

C. In the last two years, two major depressive episodes have occurred that demonstrate the temporal relationships defined by criteria A and B and no nonseasonal major depressive episodes have occurred during the same period.

D. Seasonal major depressive episodes (as described above) substantially outnumber the nonseasonal major depressive episodes that may have occurred over the individual's lifetime.

in any given season. The photoperiod of the day shortens in the fall and reaches a nadir at the winter solstice. For patients with seasonal depressions, the months of October and November are commonly associated with the beginning of a depressive episode.

Some investigators have suggested that winter depressions may be biologically related to hibernation in mammals and mediated by the effects of light on the pineal gland. This remains to be seen. However, the speculation is interesting, since seasonal depressions often have atypical features, including hypersomnia and hyperphagia.

Approximately 10 years ago, researchers began to test the theory that seasonal depression could be related to the seasonal decrease in daylight (a shortened photoperiod) by treating such patients with full spectrum light (phototherapy) in the fall and winter. Treating seasonal depression with full spectrum light in the morning and/or evening, in the fall and winter, effectively extends the photoperiod of the day and may prevent and treat some cases of seasonal depression.

Like any other specialized treatment, phototherapy is best administered by a specialist familiar with the procedure. The risks of phototherapy are low but include headaches and opthalmic damage with some light units. A typical practice is to use a specially designed, portable light box, which patients use at home for 30 minutes or more in the morning or evening. These light boxes deliver 2,500 to 10,000 lux units of full spectrum light. Patients can place the light boxes on their desks while they work in the morning or evening. The objective is to extend patients' exposure to the photoperiod.

Most trials that have demonstrated the efficacy of phototherapy in seasonal depression have been short, typically two weeks. Patients not responding to phototherapy in two weeks should probably be started on standard antidepressant treatment.

Furthermore, most patients studied with phototherapy have had mild to moderate depressive episodes. Patients with severe depressive episodes, even if they are seasonal, should be started on standard antidepressants or ECT if they meet the criteria (see Section #11). However, phototherapy may be employed as an adjunctive treatment or potential prophylaxis for subsequent episodes in patients with severe depressive episodes.

Patients with histories of bipolar disorder should probably not be treated with phototherapy alone since it, like any effective antidepressant, can induce mania in these patients. Phototherapy may be used in combination with mood-stabilizing drugs, such as lithium, in bipolar patients.

References:

Anton RF, Sexauer JD: Efficacy of amoxapine in psychotic depression. Am J Psychiatry 1983;140: 1344-1347.

Avery D, Winokur G: The efficacy of electroconvulsive therapy and antidepressants in depression. Biol Psychiatry 1977;12;507-523.

Chan CH, Janicak PG, Davis JM et al.: Response of psychotic and nonpsychotic depressed patients to tricyclic antidepressants. J Clin Psychiatry 1987;48:197-200.

Liebowitz MR, Quitkin FM, Stewart JW et al.: Antidepressant specificity in atypical depression. Arch Gen Psychiatry 1988;45:129-137.

Nelson CJ, Mazure CM, Jatlow PI: Does melancholia predict response in major depression? J Affect Disord 1990;18:157-165.

Quitkin FM, McGrath PJ, Stewart JW et al.: Phenelzine vs imipramine in mood reactive depression: Further delineation of the syndrome of atypical depression. Arch Gen Psychiatry 1989;46: 787-793.

Rosenthal NE, Bleher MC, eds.: Seasonal affective disorders and phototherapy. Guilford Press, New York, 1989.

Rosenthal NE, Sack D, Carpenter CJ et al.: Antidepressant effects of light in seasonal affective disorder. Am J Psychiatry 1985;142:163-170.

Spiker DG, Weiss JC, Dealy RS et al.: The pharmacological treatment of psychotic depression. Am J Psychiatry 1985;142:430-436.

#16 Treatment of Resistant and Recurrent Depression

Approximately 60 to 70 percent of patients have a marked response to a single trial of antidepressant medications, leaving 30 to 40 percent who are non-responders. In addition, the majority of responders to an initial antidepressant trial are not necessarily complete responders, in that many responses are incomplete (i.e., have some depressive symptoms that persist). Although there is no current consensus on what defines treatment resistance, for this discussion it will be defined as the failure of one or more adequate antidepressant trials. There are a number of important treatment considerations for treatment-resistant patients.

Switching Classes

If patients fail an adequate antidepressant trial with one class of antidepressants, it may be reasonable to try another class. This has been a popular strategy since the advent of MAOIs and tricyclic drugs; for example, if patients failed trials with tricyclic drugs, they were frequently treated with MAOIs. The strategy is based on the rationale that different classes of antidepressants have different mechanisms of action and varying effects on monoamine neurotransmitters. Since major depression appears to be a heterogeneous disorder with different pathophysiologies, some patients may respond to one class of agents and not others.

The utility of switching from a TCA to another drug class has been examined in a few case reports and studies. Failure of response with

TCAs has been followed by successful treatment with drugs from other classes, including phenelzine (Nardil), fluoxetine (Prozac), bupropion (Wellbutrin), and trazodone (Desyrel); about 50 to 65 percent of patients who fail on tricyclics respond to a second trial with antidepressants of a different class. Switching among other classes of antidepressants has been less well studied but may produce a similar response rate. It is not known what percentage of patients who fail two adequate antidepressant trials respond to a third.

Many clinicians prefer to switch classes of drugs as the first strategy after patients have failed antidepressant trials. Augmentation strategies involve adding other drugs to treatment regimens, and many clinicians feel less comfortable prescribing two or more drugs concurrently than prescribing one medication at a time. Thus, it is common among physicians to try antidepressants from two different classes before employing augmentation strategies (see Figure 16.1).

Switching to another drug within the same class is not supported by the research literature. It was quite common in years past to switch from one tricyclic to another just as it is now common to switch from one SSRI to another. Switching among various TCAs appears to yield a less than 25 percent chance of success. To this date, there is not a single study that has examined whether switching from one SSRI to another is likely to be any more successful.

Augmentation Strategies

A growing number of agents have been added to ongoing antidepressant trials to augment antidepressant response (see Table 16.1). Intuitively, it may make sense that combining agents with different neuro-transmitter effects may be useful in some patients; however, most drug combinations aimed at augmenting antidepressant effects have not been well studied.

The best studied augmenting agent for treating depression is lithium, which is used primarily in treating bipolar disorder but may have a role both in the prevention of recurrent major depression and in augmenting standard antidepressants.

Lithium has been successful in augmenting the effects of several classes of antidepressants, including the tricyclic drugs, MAOIs, and SSRIs. Typical doses for augmentation are 300 mg two or three times a day. Patients may respond to trials as short as a few days, but the most robust response has been seen with trials of three weeks or longer. Up to 65 percent of patients who are non-responders on first antidepressant trials become good responders when lithium is added to the regimen. Serum lithium levels need to be monitored regularly; levels of 0.5 to 1.0 meq/l appear adequate.

The second most studied augmentation strategy is thyroid hormone supplements. Even patients with normal thyroid levels sometime respond to small doses of levothyroxine sodium (T_4) or triiodothyronine (T_3) added to the regimen. Thyroid augmentation has been studied primarily in conjunction with tricyclics and MAOIs. Its response rate appears to be generally less robust than that of lithium augmentation, with approximately 25 to 75 percent of depressed patients reporting marked response. However, some studies have found no benefit to thyroid augmentation in euthyroid patients. Anecdotally, females over age 50, those at greatest risk for developing hypothyroidism, may be among the best responders to thyroid augmentation. Typical augmentation doses are 25 to 50 mcg of T_3 (cytomel).

Several augmenting strategies have been employed in combination with SSRIs. One involves adding buspirone (Buspar) to therapeutic doses of SSRIs. Buspirone, a partial agent of one serotonin receptor subtype (the 5-HT_1A receptor), is used primarily in treating generalized anxiety. Combining a serotonin re-uptake blocker, such as fluoxetine (Prozac), with a drug that acts directly on serotonin receptors may have synergistic antidepressants effects. A number of uncontrolled studies and case reports suggest that buspirone in divided doses of 30 to 45 mg per day may be useful in augmenting the effects of SSRIs in treating major depression and obsessive compulsive disorder. In addition, buspirone may help mitigate the sexual dysfunction associated with SSRIs.

Another serotonergic drug frequently combined with SSRIs is trazodone (Desyrel), used both to balance the CNS activation associated with SSRI use and to augment antidepressant effects. A bedtime dose of trazodone often counteracts the treatment-emergent insomnia and agitation sometimes associated with SSRIs. There is less evidence that trazodone and SSRIs are synergistic antidepressants, but some reports suggest an augmenting role for trazodone.

Finally, SSRIs are sometimes combined with more noradrenergic tricyclic drugs for augmentation purposes. SSRIs are potent serotonin reuptake blockers, while some TCAs, such as desipramine, are potent noradrenergic re-uptake blockers. Thus, the combination may have synergistic antidepressant effects. However, caution needs to be exercised in combining SSRIs with TCAs since fluoxetine (Prozac) and paroxetine (Paxil) may increase tricyclic plasma levels tenfold, resulting in serious toxicity.

The Use of ECT in Treatment-Resistant Patients

As previously described, ECT is an important option in the treatment-resistant patient (see Section #11). As many as 50 to 70 percent of patients who fail antidepressant trials respond to ECT. This is clearly a lower response rate than that seen with patients who have not failed multiple medication trials, but ECT may offer the best chance for patients with severe, treatment-resistant depression.

For patients who have failed multiple medication trials and do respond to ECT, the ongoing treatment of choice appears to be maintenance ECT, since the relapse rate in treatment-resistant depression responsive to ECT may be more than 70 percent within one year of treatment. This high relapse rate is despite adequate pharmacotherapy with antidepressants after a successful ECT series. In maintenance ECT, depressed patients are treated every few weeks or every few months and treatments may involve a single "booster" ECT treatment or a series of treatments. Maintenance treatments are frequently performed on an outpatient basis, and many severely depressed patients find tremendously improved quality of life with such treatment.

One disadvantage of maintenance ECT is the confusion and memory loss that may be sustained with frequent maintenance treatments, particularly in the elderly.

FIGURE 16.1 – Algorithm for Treatment of Resistant Depression

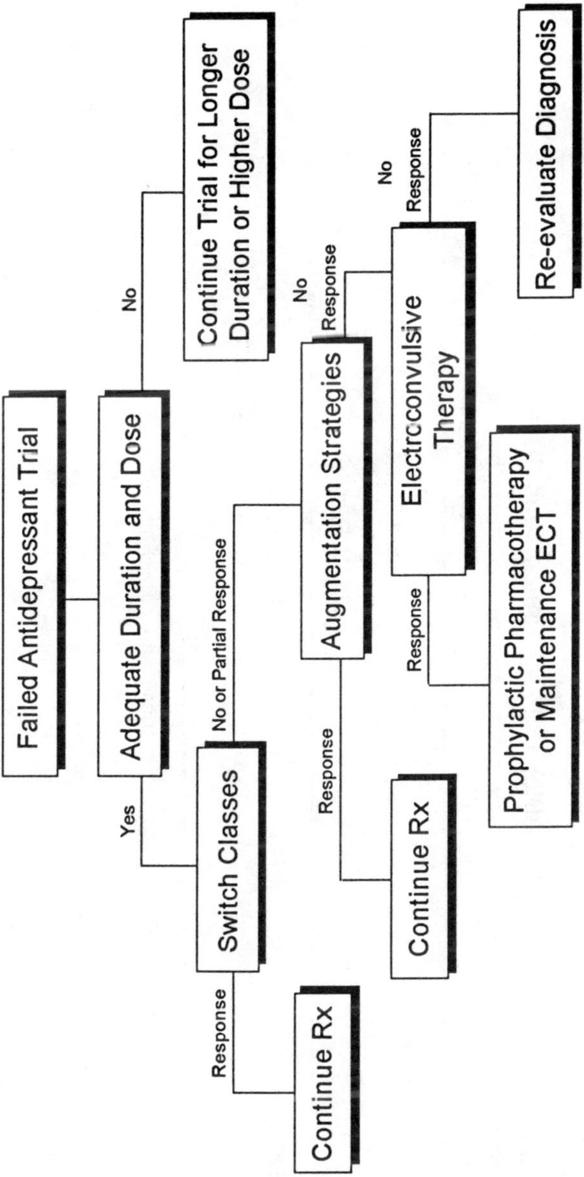

TABLE 16.1 — **Augmentation Strategies**

Antidepressants	Possible Augmenting Agents
Tricyclic/Tetracyclic	Lithium Thyroid supplements SSRIs
Monoamine Oxidase Inhibitor	Lithium Thyroid supplements (may be less effective than combining with TCAs)
Selective Serotonin Re-uptake Inhibitors	Lithium Buspirone (Buspar) Trazodone (Desyrel) TCAs

Diagnostic Considerations

If patients continue to be resistant to various, adequate treatment strategies, careful re-evaluation of the diagnosis is essential. Attention should be focused on co-morbid medical conditions (see Section #2), and a careful examination of concurrent medications should be undertaken.

The possibility that treatment-resistant patients have a treatable subtype of depression should also be reviewed (see Section #15). This may be particularly important for psychotic depression in which only 20 to 30 percent of patients respond to antidepressants alone. The psychotic symptoms also may be quite subtle. For example, in geriatric patients, the line between over-concern about physical health and a somatic delusion may be quite blurry; in such patients, the possibility of combination therapy with antipsychotic agents and ECT should be considered.

Co-morbid psychiatric conditions also increase the possibility of treatment resistance. Concurrent substance abuse is a frequent confounding factor; treatment-resistant depressed patients should be asked about their alcohol intake and any substance abuse. If underlying substance abuse problems are detected, these problems should be treated aggressively, since antidepressant treatment alone is unlikely to be effective.

Severe personality disorders such as borderline personality are frequently associated with symptoms of depression. While antidepressants may relieve some depressive features of these patients, euthymia (mental peace) is often elusive. Long-term psychosocial therapy is generally the treatment of choice.

Treatment of Recurrent Major Depression

At least 50 to 85 percent of patients with one major depressive episode will have another. For many patients, major depression is a chronic illness with exacerbations and remissions. A history of previous episodes and concurrent psychiatric or substance abuse problems substantially increase the risk of recurrence. Several studies suggest that long-term treatment can substantially reduce the risk of recurrences for these patients. In fact, the risk of recurrence appears to be three to six times higher for patients with a history of recurrence who continue antidepressant treatment than for those taking placebo.

The treatment of recurrent depression is usually divided into three stages. Antidepressant trials are initiated in the acute stage and continue until substantial or complete remission of symptoms occurs. This stage usually lasts the four to 12 weeks required for antidepressants to become effective. The second stage, preventing relapse, is the continuation phase during which antidepressants are continued for at least 20 additional weeks regardless of patients' histories of recurrence. Discontinuing treatment prematurely substantially increases risks of relapse. In the last stage, the maintenance phase, the goal is preventing recurrence. The maintenance stage is long-term. Many patients are candidates for maintenance antidepressants (see Table 16.2); and for some patients with severe, debilitating recurrences, maintenance therapy may be a lifetime commitment.

Most antidepressants studied appear to be effective in the preventing recurrences. Long-term studies (two to five years) have shown signifi-

TABLE 16.2 – **Candidates for Maintenance of Antidepressant Therapy**	
❶	Patients with a history of two severe episodes in the last five years
❷	Patients with a history of recurrence within two years of discontinuing antidepressant treatment
❸	Patients with three or more lifetime episodes of major depression

cant prophylactic effects of TCA drugs, including imipramine (Tofranil), amitriptyline (Elavil), doxepin (Sinequan), and nortriptyline (Pamelor). Long-term use of the MAOI phenelzine (Nardil) also has been shown to reduce recurrences substantially. Studies of SSRIs and venlafaxine (Effexor) have typically been for just one year, but these drugs appear to be as effective as the older agents in preventing recurrences. Finally, lithium appears to be useful in preventing recurrences in patients with mild to moderate major depressive episodes and as effective as the other antidepressants (usually imipramine [Tofranil]) it has been compared with in maintenance studies. However, patients with severe recurrences may do less well on lithium alone.

Doses required for effective prophylaxis in the maintenance phase are the same doses required to obtain remission in the acute phase. It used to be common to prescribe a reduced dose to limit side effects after remission has occurred, but the current data suggest that this appears to be a mistake. Patients treated with reduced doses during the maintenance phase have a higher rate of recurrence than those on full antidepressant doses.

Psychotherapy also holds promise in preventing recurrences. There are data that the skills learned in cognitive-behavioral therapy and interpersonal psychotherapy may mitigate the risks of recurrence. However, in some studies, interpersonal psychotherapy with placebo was more effective than placebo alone at preventing recurrences but much less effective than imipramine (Tofranil) alone.

Patients with recurrent major depression present a significant therapeutic challenge. Such patients should be reassured that a variety of treatment options appears to be useful, including maintenance antidepressants, maintenance ECT, and psychotherapy.

References:

Beasley CM, Sayler ME, Cunningham GE et al.: Fluoxetine in tricyclic refractory major depressive disorder. J Affect Disorders 1990;20:193-200.

Fink M: Electroconvulsive therapy: The forgotten option in the treatment of therapy resistant depression. In: Treatment of tricyclic resistant depression. Extein IL, ed. APA press, Washington, DC, 1989.

Frank E, Kupfer E, Perel JM et al.: Three-year outcomes for maintenance therapies in recurrent depression. Arch Gen Psychiatry 1990;47:1093-1099.

Jacobsen FM: Possible augmentation of antidepressant response by buspirone. J Clin Psychiatry 1991;52:217-220.

Joffe RT, Singer W: Thyroid hormone potentiation of antidepressants. In: Refractory depression. Amsterdam JD, ed. Raven Press, New York, 1991.

Keller MB: The difficult depressed patient in perspective. J Clin Psychiatry Feb. 1993;54(2) Suppl:4-9.

Kupfer DJ, Frank E, Perl JM et al.: Five-year outcomes for maintenance therapies in recurrent depression. Arch Gen Psychiatry 1992;49:769-773.

Nierenberg AA: A systematic approach to treatment resistant depression. J Clin Psychiatry, monograph series 1992;10(1):5-9.

Nierenberg AA, Amsterdam JD: Treatment resistant depression: Definition and treatment approaches. J Clin Psychiatry 1990;51(6)Suppl:39-47.

Prien RF, Kupfer DJ: Continuation therapy for major depression: How long should it be maintained? Am J Psychiatry 1986;143:18-23.

Prien RF, Kupfer DJ, Mansky PA et al.: Drug therapy in the prevention of recurrences in unipolar and bipolar affective disorders. Report of the NIMH Collaborative Study Group Comparing Lithium Carbonate, Imipramine, and Lithium Carbonate-Imipramine Combinations. Arch Gen Psychiatry 1984;41:1096-1104.

Weilburg JB, Rosenbaum JF, Biederman J et al.: Fluoxetine added to non-MAOIs converts nonresponders to responders: A preliminary report. J Clin Psychiatry 1989;50:447-449.

Appendix

Antidepressant Drug Interactions

Drug Interaction	SSRIs	TCAs	MAOIs	5 HT-2 Antagonist	Venlafaxine	Bupropion
TCAs	Increase TCA levels-arrhythmia	NA	Serotonin syndrome with clomipramin and increase hypotension	Increase hypotension	Unknown	May increase seizure risk
MAOIs	Serotonin syndrome	Serotonin syndrome (mostly with clomipramine) and increase hypotension	NA	Increase hypotension, Serotonin syndrome (some risk)	Serotonin syndrome	Hypertensive crisis
Venlafaxine	Clinical significance unknown	Unknown	Serotonin syndrome	Unknown	NA	Unknown

SSRIs	NA	Increase TCA levels arrhythmia	Serotonin syndrome	May increase dysphoric activation by increasing CPP	Limited known interaction	One report of seizure, but generally limited interaction
Bupropion	Unknown One report of seizure	Combination may increase risk of seizure	Hyperten-sive crisis	Unknown	Limited known interaction	NA
Ca Channel Blockers diltiazem nifedipine verapamil	Fluvoxamine may significantly increase levels	TCAs may moderately increase levels	Increase hypotension	Nefazodone may significantly increase levels	Limited known interaction	Limited known interaction
ß-Blockers propranolol timolol metoprolol	May increase ß-Blocker levels and hypotension	Increase hypotension	Increase hypotension	Increase hypotension	Limited known interaction	Unknown

Antidepressant Drug Interactions (continued)

Drug Interaction	SSRIs	TCAs	MAOIs	5 HT-2 Antagonist	Venlafaxine	Bupropion
Caffeine Theophylline	Fluvoxamine significantly increases levels	TCAs may slightly increase levels	Risk of hypertensive crisis	May slightly increase levels	Limited known interaction	Unknown
Anti-Psychotics risperidone clozapine perphenazine	Increase antipsychotic levels	May increase antipsychotic levels	Increase hypotension	Increase hypotension	Limited known interaction	May exacerbate psychosis
1-C Anti-arrhythmics flecainide encainide	Significant increase 1-C levels and arrhythmias	Secondary Amines may moderately increase risk of arrhythmia	Unknown	Nefazodone may slightly increase levels	Limited known interaction	Limited known interaction

Terfenadine **Astemizole** **Cisapride**	Fluvoxamine may increase risk of arrhythmia (Torsades)	TCAs may slightly increase levels (NCS)	Unknown	Nefazodone significantly increases risk of Torsades arrhythmia	Limited known interaction	Limited known interaction
Triazolo- **Benzos** **alprazolam** **triazolam** **midazolam**	Fluvoxamine Signifiant increase benzo levels (others slightly)	TCAs slightly increase levels and sedation	May increase sedation	Nefazodone significantly increases levels	Limited known interaction	Limited known interaction
Warfarin **Tolbutamide** **Dilantin**	Fluvoxamine fluoxetine may increase levels	Limited known interaction	Unknown	Limited known interaction	Limited known interaction	Limited known interaction

– ABBREVIATIONS –

ACE	Angiotensin Converting Enzyme
BDI	Beck Depression Inventory
BUN	Blood Urea Nitrogen
CBC	Complete Blood Count
CBT	Cognitive-Behavioral Therapy
CNS	Central Nervous System
DSM IV	Diagnostic and Statistical Manual of Psychiatric Disorders
DST	Dexamethasone Suppression Test
ECT	Electroconvulsive Therapy
GI	Gastrointestinal
Ham-D	Hamilton Depression Scale
HPA	Hypothalamic Pituitary Axis
IPT	Interpersonal Psychotherapy
MAOI	Monoamine Oxidase Inhibitor
MCV	Mean Corpuscular Volume
OCD	Obsessive Compulsive Disorder
SNRI	Selective Serotonin Norepinephrine Re-uptake Inhibitor
SSRI	Selective Serotonin Re-uptake Inhibitors
TCA	Tricyclic Antidepressant
TRH	Thyrotropin Releasing Hormone
TRHST	Thyrotropin Releasing Hormone Stimulation Test
TSH	Thyroid Stimulating Hormone

NOTES

Index

– OTHER CENTER INDEX PUBLICATIONS –

REPRODUCTIVE HEALTH

Breastfeeding: *A Problem-Solving Manual* - 4th ed. — Saunders, Carroll & Johnson
Contraceptive Surgery for Men and Women - 2nd ed. — Moss/AVSC
Endometriosis: *The Enigmatic Disease* — Corson
Family Planning at Your Fingertips — Hatcher, et al
Gynecological Care Manual for HIV Positive Women — Denenberg
Management of Infertility: *A Clinician's Manual* - 2nd ed. — Cohen
Menopause: Clinical Concepts - 2nd ed. - London & Chihal
Managing Danazol Patients - 2nd ed. — Dickey
Hormone Replacement Therapy - 4th ed. — Gambrell
Oral Contraceptive User Guide - 2nd ed. — Dickey
Safe Sex: *A Guide to Condoms* - 2nd ed. — Brackett

CARDIOLOGY

Cholesterol Treatment: *User Guide to Lipid Disorder Management* - 2nd ed. — Leaf
Emergency Cardiac Maneuvers - 2nd ed. — Bartecchi
Hypertension Treatment User Guide - 2nd ed. — Kaplan
Management of Heart Failure — Cohn & Kubo
Management of Hypertension - 6th ed. — Kaplan

GENERAL MEDICINE

A Manual on Drug Dependence — Nahas
A Practical Anesthesia Information Guide — Jerome
Arthritis Therapy: *A Clinician's Manual* — Kantor
Assessment and Management of the Suicidal Adolescent - Clayton
Breast Disease in Women and Men — Shuler
Handbook of Headache Disorders - 2nd ed. — Elkind
Management of Aneurysmal Subarachnoid Hemorrhage — Fosset
Management of Diabetes Mellitus - 3rd ed. — Schwartz & Schwartz
Medical Management of Depression - DeBattista & Glick
Mid-Life Sexuality: *Enrichment and Problem Solving* — Semmens
Projective Psychodiagnostic Assessment — Caldwell & Dixon
Primary Mental Health Care — Behrman✱

EDUCATION

Accelerated Learning: *How You Learn Determines What You Learn* — Swartz
Chief Executive Officer's Guide for Health Facility Development - 2nd ed. — Weeks
Children with Special Needs - 2nd ed. — Bradway & Block
Infection Prevention for Family Planning Service Programs — Tietjen, Cronin & McIntosh (JHPIEGO) ✱
Resilience Enhancement for the Resident Physician — Messner✱
Travel Well: *a gourmet guide to healthy travel* — Kaplan ✱

✱Not Center-Indexed Publications

Lourdes Library
Gwynedd Mercy College
P. O. Box 901
Gwynedd Valley, PA 19437-0901